Lecture Notes in Artificial Intelligence   1056

Subseries of Lecture Notes in Computer Science
Edited by J. G. Carbonell and J. Siekmann

Lecture Notes in Computer Science

Edited by G. Goos, J. Hartmanis and J. van Leeuwen

Springer
Berlin
Heidelberg
New York
Barcelona
Budapest
Hong Kong
London
Milan
Paris
Santa Clara
Singapore
Tokyo

Afsaneh Haddadi

Communication and Cooperation in Agent Systems

A Pragmatic Theory

Springer

Series Editors

Jaime G. Carbonell
School of Computer Science, Carnegie Mellon University
Pittsburgh, PA 15213-3891, USA

Jörg Siekmann
University of Saarland
German Research Center for Artificial Intelligence (DFKI)
Stuhlsatzenhausweg 3, D-66123 Saarbrücken, Germany

Author

Afsaneh Haddadi
Daimler-Benz AG, Center for Research and Technology
Alt-Moabit 96a, D-10559 Berlin, Germany

Cataloging-in-Publication Data applied for

Die Deutsche Bibliothek - CIP-Einheitsaufnahme

Haddadi, Afsaneh:
Communication and cooperation in agent systems : a pragmatic
theory / Afsaneh Haddadi. - Berlin ; Heidelberg ; New York ;
Barcelona ; Budapest ; Hong Kong ; London ; Milan ; Paris ;
Santa Clara ; Singapore ; Tokyo : Springer, 1996
  (Lecture notes in computer science ; 1056 : Lecture notes in artificial
  intelligence)
  ISBN 3-540-61044-8
NE: GT

CR Subject Classification (1991): I.2.11, I.2, D.2.7, C.2.4, H.3.5

ISBN 3-540-61044-8 Springer-Verlag Berlin Heidelberg New York

Typesetting: Camera ready by author
SPIN 10512790   06/3142 – 5 4 3 2 1 0   Printed on acid-free paper

To the COSY team

Preface

Rapid and increasing advances in telecommunications and distributed systems have broadened the arena of research in challenging applications such as electronic markets, distributed intelligent information services, distributed manufacturing control, cooperative multi-robot applications, and many more. These advances have enabled access to a wide variety of communication networks, offering various means for logically or geographically distributed nodes to connect and communicate. Ever increasing speed in communication, as well as new technologies enabling import and export of program codes for execution on the networks, is making rapid, real-time, interactive communication among the nodes a growing reality.

With these possibilities, real challenges are converging on problems requiring better software engineering solutions. As programs are becoming more sophisticated, they may collaborate and negotiate with other programs in order to achieve their assigned tasks. To do this they may need to communicate more intelligibly and exhibit sufficient flexibility to build up their dialogues dynamically and interactively. This has been one of the critical lines of research in the field of Multi-Agent Systems (MAS). Typically agents are computational programs inhabiting dynamic and unpredictable environments. They are equipped with sensoric and effectoric capabilities, and some internal processing component that relates the sensoric events to appropriate actions effecting the environment. Agents have a sufficient degree of decision-making autonomy and can only interact with other agents by explicit communication. The ability to perform intelligent dialogues is particularly crucial when we have an open system where (heterogeneous) agents "enter and leave" the system with little or no information about each other's capabilities.

This book presents an approach towards the specification and design of techniques enabling intelligent and flexible dialogues between agents in distributed environments. The approach motivates the idea that agents should reason about communication and they should do this as part of their general reasoning about actions. The focus of the work is on cooperation, and communication in this context is therefore considered as an integral part of reasoning about cooperation.

But how could one model an agent so that it could effectively reason about its actions and its interactions with other agents? This book follows the long tradition in artificial intelligence which suggests modelling an agent as having mental states such as beliefs and desires, and reasoning in terms of transition between these states. This approach has been influenced by the folk psychological explanation of human behaviour. For instance an agent's reasoning about its actions may be explained in terms of what it believes to be true in a given situation, what it aims to achieve, and how best it could achieve those aims. This is also the perspective taken in the philosophical explanation of *rational* behaviour, and is generally referred to as an *intentional stance*. To reason about communication and cooperation an agent may reciprocate the instance and model another agent as also being an intentional system. Motivated by this approach, a formalism is developed in this book to describe the relations between a subset of intentional attitudes, namely, *beliefs, desires,* and *intentions* (BDI) which are increasingly accepted as playing an important role in the design of practical agent architectures.

For "meaningful" communication agents need to understand the messages exchanged. The studies in speech act theory have had a considerable impact in this area. The most significant is the idea that by uttering a sentence the speaker is performing an action, intending to bring about some effect on the hearer. The action of this communication is referred to as a *speech act*. Therefore reasoning about communication is in effect the process of reasoning about which speech act to perform. A pragmatic approach to reasoning about these actions is to give their semantics and specify their pre- and post-conditions of execution. This way communicative actions can be reasoned about and selected like other actions as in planning systems for instance.

This book presents the first attempt to give the formal semantics of speech acts in a BDI logic. The formalism is based on a variant of Rao and Georgeff's BDI logics and describes it in some depth. The work is shaped around the idea that before engaging in cooperation agents may have to communicate their beliefs and desires, and negotiate on how they wish to cooperate. The main incentive for negotiation is to arrive at an agreement and make a joint commitment. Therefore a theory of joint commitments is developed which draws together various components of practical reasoning.

Using this theory, the approach demonstrates how in practice agents may reason about and build up the steps of their dialogue dynamically. The most important practical benefit of this approach is that agents' interactions within a particular context can be compiled into high-level plans of dialogues known as *cooperation protocols*. Cooperation protocols provide a mechanism to express various methods of cooperation and possible patterns of dialogue in those methods. They provide the interacting agents with a guideline as how the dialogue may proceed and when to reason about what and with which agents to communicate.

This book draws together many ideas on speech acts, cooperation, dialogues and agent architectures, and as a result may be useful to many disciplines concerned with intelligent systems and intelligent behaviours. In particular the book is intended to benefit those interested in high-level languages for inter-agent communication and flexible dialogues. The incentives for this work, and the literature review material provided in the introductory chapters will be useful to those starting in the field of agent systems and agent theories. The book also makes references to the existing architectures for intentional agents and evaluates them in the context of this work.

A broad range of topics have been covered, each topic deserving a much more thorough and deeper analysis than that presented here. This book is but an attempt to characterise the main components requisite to the design of practical agent architectures that support intelligent communication, and demonstrate how various influencing factors may be integrated into a unified framework. It is the hope of the author that the material presented in this book motivates further research in this area.

February 1996   Afsaneh Haddadi

Table of Contents

1. Introduction

1.1 Overview

The recent years have witnessed a large interest in "*agent-oriented*" approaches to developing systems. These approaches have been very diverse. Although in general "autonomy", and at times *communication capabilities* are mentioned as important attributes, there seems to be no commonly agreed properties that characterise a system as an agent, either from the outset, or from its constituting components. While side-stepping the debates that have resulted on these issues, the standpoint taken in this book is that of "*agents as intentional systems*".

As the application domains being considered are becoming increasingly large and complex, at times one is urged to appeal to a level of abstraction at which the problem and its solution could be expressed more naturally. Intentional attitudes, usually attributed to human (at least psychologically) appear to provide just the right level of abstraction. One could express an agent's problem-solving mechanism in terms of what it[1] may believe, how it may go about achieving its goals and wishes, what capabilities it possesses, and relate its behaviour to its individual characteristics and attributes like its preferences. By appealing to Dennett's philosophy of "*ladder of personhood*" [Den81], one could go beyond this and describe an agent with increasing levels of sophistication, one that could reciprocate on it's own intentional attitudes and those of other agents, one that could "rationally" communicate with other agents and even one that possesses some level of consciousness.

Section 1.2 sets the background to the notion of intentional systems and Section 1.3 provides various classifications of intentional attitudes in relation to their role in rational behaviour of computational systems. Having motivated the concept of agents as intentional systems, Section 1.4 will outline the purpose, the approach, and the structure of this book.

---

[1] Throughout this book, different pronouns (i.e., he, she, it) are used interchangeably to refer to an agent.

1.2 Intentional Systems

When describing human behaviour, we make use of terms such as 'feeling', 'wanting', 'believing', etc., which stem from the folk psychological or common sense understanding we have in explaining the observable properties of mind. Dennett [Den81] refers to this as *intentional explanation*. An example of intentional explanation is: "He threw himself to the floor because he thought that the gun was loaded" (c. f. [Nar91]).

In an attempt to develop a theory of *Intentionality*, Searle states:

> "*Intentionality is that property of many mental states and events by which they are directed at or about or of objects and states of affairs in the world. If, for example, I have a belief it must be a belief that such and such is the case; ...if I have a desire, it must be the desire to do something or that something should happen or be the case; if I have an intention, it must be an intention to do something. ...I follow a long philosophical tradition in calling this feature of directedness or aboutness "Intentionality"...only some, not all, mental states and event have Intentionality. Beliefs, fears, and desires are Intentional; but there are forms of nervousness, elation, and undirected anxiety that are not Intentional.*" [Sea83]

Dennett chooses to refer to these attitudes as *intentions*[2] instead of *intentionality*. However, *intentionality* constitutes the second condition in his ladder of personhood where it refers to the "*ascription to the system of beliefs and desires*".

There is yet another related term, i.e. *intention* which is one form of Intentionality/intentions. The use of this term has been rather diverse, but in general it refers to a choice/decision and a commitment/persistence on that choice.

By far, the best account of intentional systems is given by Dennett [Den81]. Although he is mainly concerned with "moral personhood" than personhood *per se*, he states:

> "*Intentional explanations have the action of persons as their primary domain, but there are times when we find intentional explanations (and predictions based on them) not only useful but indispensable for accounting for the behaviour of complex machines*" ([Den81], pages 236-237)

A comprehensive account of this philosophical framework is given by Narayanan in his second volume of *On Being a Machine* [Nar91], and the

---

[2] *Intention-with-t* should not be confused with *intension-with-s*. The latter's English meaning belongs to the family of intentness and intensity; and in logic it refers to all qualities or properties which a term or concept signifies: opposed to *extension*. [Webster's Dictionary]

material presented here is an adaptation of the 5th chapter of this book. Dennett's ladder of personhood which appears in his article *Brainstorm* [Den81], consists of six conditions:

- rationality
- intentionality
- stance
- reciprocity
- communication
- consciousness

The first three are mutually interdependent and are used for defining a *basic intentional system*.

Intentionality refers to the system's intentions as rationally following from its beliefs about the world and from its high level preferences. This requires the modelling of the entities in the world in an appropriate level which brings us to the third condition: *stance*. Dennett distinguishes three categories: *physical stance* refers to modeling entities based on the information of their physical state together with knowledge of the laws of nature; *design stance* refers to modeling entities based on the information of their functionality; and *intentional stance* refers to modeling a system as an intentional system, i.e. as having beliefs, intentions and so forth (at least from the outset). Prediction from intentional stance assumes rationality by the system, but not necessarily perfect rationality. Here one can see the interdependency of *intentionality* condition and the intentional *stance*.

Dennett's account of *rationality* is somewhat loose. He unpacks the condition in two ways by appealing to the *rules of logic*, and by providing some sort of status for the beliefs that a rational being holds. With regards to the former he states:

> "... *one gets nowhere with the assumption that entity x has beliefs p , q , r , ... unless one also supposes that x believes what follows from p , q , r , ...* "

And with respect to the latter, he imposes two conditions:

> " ... *(1) In general, normally, more often than not, if x believes p, p is true. (2) In general, normally, more often than not, if x avows that p, he believes p [and, by (1), p is true].*"[3]

The subject of rationality has been studied in the psychological and philosophical studies of human behaviour and in Decision Theory which will be discussed in some detail in Section 2.5.

Whereas the first three conditions are mutually interdependent and they are not ordered, the remaining conditions are ordered. The fourth condition:

---

[3] The 'normative' aspects of Dennett's theory have been criticised on the grounds that under such an account, one can always impose an agent to have certain beliefs. (For more discussions see [Nar91], pages 23-25.)

reciprocity is the capacity in intentional systems to exhibit higher-order intentions, and while it is dependent on the first three conditions, is independent of the fifth and the sixth. To clarify this condition, Narayanan further explains that:

> " ... *a person should reciprocate the stance, and this is best achieved by requiring that an intentional system itself adopts the intentional stance towards other objects. This in turn is best achieved by allowing an intentional system to ascribe beliefs, desires and intentions about beliefs, desires and intentions.*"

In effect, reciprocity is a recursive nesting of intentionality [GD93][4].

The next condition is the ability for meaningful *communication*. Gmytrasiewicz and Durfee note that communication is related to the notion of reciprocity since in order to effectively communicate, an agent has to consider how its utterances are used by the hearer to update its beliefs, including the beliefs about the speaker's beliefs and so on. And then they describe a "meaningful" act of communication as the ability to judge what messages should be sent, to whom, and in what way, given a particular situation, that is, *"the ability of a communicative behaviour"*. In fact, this step nicely captures the essence of the work presented in this book and will be discussed in more detail in the next chapter.

Finally, the last condition on the ladder is *consciousness* which refers to the agent's ability to modify its own high level preferences [Den91]. This could be related to systems with learning and adapting capabilities. This condition will not be considered any further in this work.

The folk psychological approaches, (i.e., ascription of mental propositions or intentionality to a system), have received criticisms from different sides. Most noticeable are due to Patricia and Paul Churchland [Chu88][CST92], who object to the non-scientific principal of observational conception of notions like 'feeling', 'believing', 'intending' etc., claiming that the folk psychological theories will eventually be displaced by a "completed" neuroscience. According to Paul Churchland's theory (known as *eliminative materialism*), a detailed neuro physiological-based understanding of ourselves (a materialistic understanding) will eventually displace (eliminate) our current mentalistic self-conception, [Chu81]. Patricia Churchland [CST92] notes:

> "... *in the evolution of science, it appears highly probable that psychological processes are in fact processes of the physical brain, not, processes of a non-physical soul or mind.*"

Hence they argue for study of the brain from its micro-structure to its macro-structure to get clues about how artificially "intelligent" or "autonomous" systems should be designed and developed. Along the same lines, Tim Smithers [Smi91] rejects the folk psychological influences in AI, arguing

---

[4] See next chapter Section 2.6.1 for *nested beliefs* and *mutual beliefs*.

that its implicit use and the lack of awareness of the practitioners of this use, is the blame for the lack of measurable success in AI.

Though such criticisms appear to be well-grounded, it is still debatable if the theory of intentional stance should be completely abandoned. From a thorough examination of Dennett's theory, it is hard to see it as contradicting the theory of materialism. His stress is more on the explanation and prediction of behaviours anyway. However, it is entirely a different matter when the influence of such a theory [alone] on the design and construction of autonomous systems is being questioned.

It seems that the cause for the long debate on the subject of "folk psychology vs cognitive Science" is the failure to acknowledge that the two schools of thought are concerned with different aspects of "intelligent" behaviour, which indeed at times overlap. Cognitive Science and in particular neuroscience is concerned with the minutiae of cognition and at least currently does not necessarily need to make any attempt to integrate with social and cultural studies of people [see [PC95]). Cognitive Science to the study of mind and brain is what Biology is to the study of body and physical functions. The domain of folk psychology on the other hand is concerned with providing arguments for human "conscious" thought and "deliberation" in behaving in certain way. This may take into account also the cultural, sociological, or anthropological influences.

With respect to computational systems, these domains can still fulfill their purpose by modeling the intended systems without taking the other domain into account. For instance practitioners in neuroscience model a system to study how a certain "complex" behaviour arises from a particular interconnection of very simple function cells. On the other hand, a rational behaviour for instance may be studied by modeling the system in terms of the interaction of intentional attitudes taken as abstract components. Though for more sophisticated systems it seems inevitable that the two domains should progressively merge.

In support of intentional systems, Singh [Sin95] for instance, argues that the intentional stance makes available abstractions such as the intentions and know-how of agents and the communication that takes place among them:

> "In addition to the fact that these abstractions no doubt have much conceptual appeal, there are simple pragmatic and technical reasons for considering them seriously. They (i) are natural to us, as designers and analysers; (ii) provide succinct descriptions of, and help understand and explain, the behaviour of complex systems; (iii) make available certain regularities and patterns of action that are independent of the exact physical implementation of the agents in the system; and (iv) may be used by the agents themselves in reasoning about each other." ([Sin95])

Smithers criticises the intentional stance because it fails to offer a non-arbitrary account of how the mental states relate to brain states. This is currently true and it is our hope that the studies in biological science, neuro-science, neurocomputation and the related fields would be able to make this connection in the future. Although the enormous prospects of such studies remain undebatable, as far as design of an entity with perceivably "higher level" complex behaviours is concerned, the current advances and techniques offered by the materialism approach, have a long way to mature.

In view of current advances of each school of thought, integration in the form of hierarchical hybrid systems for instance, is seen as desirable if not inevitable. The design and engineering of more sophisticated systems, would indeed have to take both theories into account. For instance, how mental atti-tudes as we perceive them now, would emerge from millions of interconnected (artificial) neurons. This is especially true for systems (such as navigating robots) which are expected to exhibit or simulate human-like capabilities. In this book however, we will take the intentional stance for the remainder of this work.

1.3 Intentional Attitudes

Intentional attitudes seem to play different roles, some are well understood and some not. Kiss [Kis92] classifies them into three groups *cognitives, cona-tives* and *affectives*, examples of which are given in Table 1.1. Interestingly enough, Webster's Dictionary also makes pointers from each category to the other two categories. *Cognitives* refer to epistemic issues in general. *Conatives* refer to action and control, denoting an attempt to perform an action. The meaning of *conation* is *"the conscious drive to perform apparently volitional acts with or without knowledge of the origin of the drive"*. Kiss uses the term *affectives* to refer to those attitudes which correspond to the dynamics of an agent's behaviour. Hence he puts 'goal' , 'desire' and 'preference' under this category. In the Webster's dictionary however, *affective* means *"relating to, arising from, or influencing feelings or emotions"* and 'interest', 'responsibil-ity' and 'hope' are associated with this category.

Table 1.1. Kiss's classification of intentional attitudes

Cognitive	belief, knowledge, awareness
Conative	intention, commitment, plan
affective	goal, desire, preference

Shoham and Cousins [SC94], divide intentional attitudes, according to their relevance to computational applications. These are: *informational, motivational, social* and other emotions. Examples of each class are given in Table 1.2. *Informational* attitudes like *conatives* concern the information available to agents. There is a whole body of work dealing with informational attitudes and the meaning of these attitudes is largely understood (see next chapter Section 2.3). The *motivational attitudes "are in some sense directly linked to the agent's selecting one among the various possible actions available to it"* [SC94]. The authors rightly observe that although some attitudes are better understood by now than the others, the meaning of motivational terms is far less clear than those for knowledge and belief, (see next chapter, Section 2.4). The third category, *social* attitudes relates to the motivational attitudes, but gives social, moral, and/or rational reasons for behaving in a certain way (see Section 2.6). With regards to other emotions such as 'fear', 'joy' and so forth, they note that their relation to computational applications is not as yet obvious.

Table 1.2. Shoham & Cousin's classification of intentional attitudes

Informational	belief, knowledge, awareness
Motivational	intention, choice, plan goal, desire, commitment, preference, wish, want
Social	obligation, permission

Having some general impression of various classes of intentional attitudes, we need to know their role as input to the rational behaviour of agents. Motivated by Dennett's interpretation of rationality which refers to the quality of following the rules of logic, we will study the logical formalisms employed to model these attitudes in the next chapter.

1.4 The Objectives and Outline of this Book

This section first outlines the objectives of this book and then describes the approach taken, by building a background and positioning the objectives and the approach with respect to the related works.

1.4.1 The Objectives

The main purpose of this book is to study how computational agents may reason about their interactions in order to engage in a cooperation. In attempt to achieve this purpose, a number of secondary objectives are set out below:

1. Study how agents may reason about their actions and achieving their local tasks, in terms of their intentional attitudes, and whether communicative actions of agents can be derived as part of this reasoning process.
2. Develop a formal theory that captures the characteristic properties of the attitudes *beliefs, desires*, and *intentions* which play distinct roles in this process.
3. Based on the key data structures identified and defined in the theory, develop a logical specification of the conditions that lead to appropriate communicative actions of the agents involved.
4. Demonstrate how the specification of the reasoning about interactions may be modelled in an existing agent architecture, which supports reasoning about actions in terms of the key data structures defined in the theory.

This work is primarily motivated with developing methods and techniques for modelling agent-oriented systems and their applications. A closely related study in the literature, is concerned with issues related to developing agent-oriented programming languages [Sho93]. Some of the studies in this direction aim at developing programming languages that in one way or another *execute* an agent specification language. Although this book acknowledges some of these works as future research directions in chapter 6, it does not deal with the execution issues in the approach.

1.4.2 The Approach

To study how computational agents may reason about their interactions in order to engage in a cooperation, we primarily consider how agents reason about their actions in general. By taking an intentional stance, the reasoning process of an agent may be described in terms of the interplay of its intentional attitudes. There is a whole body of work in Philosophy, Cognitive Science, Computer Science, Linguistics, Computational Linguistics, Psychology, Sociology, Speech Act Theory and so on, which have aimed to capture the role of various attitudes in the rational behaviour of agents. In relation to computational systems, these studies either tend to provide theoretical analyses, or design and implement prototypes which in one way or another make use of these abstractions. The problem is that the formal theories are so complex that it is hard to see their direct relation to practice. On the other hand, the design of implemented systems is somewhat ad hoc, with hardly any theoretical foundation to justify them. There have been some attempts to relate the theories to their practical implementation, but usually this relation is only loosely defined.

In this book we aim to make this gap narrower. Following the tradition of the software development life cycle, in general, developing a program involves *requirement analysis, global design, specification, implementation, testing,* and *maintenance* [vV93]. In terms of this rather simplistic view of software development, the approach taken in this work roughly involves the first three phases. For the requirements analysis of general reasoning mechanisms of agents we rely on Bratman's philosophical analysis ([Bra87] and [Bra90]) of the triple *beliefs, desires, and intentions* (BDI), and the studies that in one way or another have been influenced by his work. These requirements are captured in a formal theory which describes the interrelationship between these attitudes. Based on this theory, the reasoning about interactions is specified in a set of rules comparable to the temporal logic specification of concurrent programs. The logical framework employed is largely identical to Rao and Georgeff's framework [RG91c], and is used as a tool to both develop the theory and outline the conditions related to the specification rules.

The basics of the the theory inherit many properties of Rao and Georgeff's BDI-system. But the BDI-system is developed to capture the requirements of the reasoning mechanism of single-agent systems 'situated' in dynamic environments. Therefore, taking this model as the basis, the theory developed in this book attempts to capture the extra requirements related to the reasoning about interactions with other agents. In single-agent systems reasoning about actions involves (i) *task selection* (what to do), (ii) *means-end reasoning* (how to do), and (iii) *execution* (when to do), while taking into account that the environment changes and therefore the decisions made in one situation may be ruled out in another situation. This has motivated many lines of research attempting to characterise the conditions for persistence on the selected tasks and the selected means of accomplishing those tasks. These are referred to as *commitment to chosen desired ends* and *commitment to chosen means* or plans of reaching those ends.

In multi-agent systems, the changes, the choices and the possibilities extend as a result of the presence of other agents in the system. Agents may have to co-exist because they share the same environment and require the same resources. On the other hand, they can also cooperate to achieve tasks that cannot be achieved by a single agent or that achieving them cooperatively would produce a better overall performance. Cooperation can range from simple delegation of a task from one agent to another, to collaborative actions of agents coordinating and synchronising their actions. In order to be able to negotiate about whether and how to cooperate, agents need to coordinate their knowledge [HB94]. If the internal states of agents are local to them, coordination of knowledge necessitates communication.

This work focuses on delegation of achievement of a task from one agent to another. Since we aim at designing agents that themselves could reason about their actions and interactions, it is important that the theory takes an *internal perspective*. In this view, the theory must specify both how an agent would go about delegating one of his own tasks, and why an agent should decide to adopt the achievement of another agent's task. This distinction is important since the reasoning strategies are different according to which role the agent plays in the interaction. This distinction is made not only in the theory but also in the specification rules and when modelling the interactions during the design phase.

Cooperation can only commence after the agents have come to an agreement and made a *commitment* to one another that they will indeed cooperate on the agreed terms. As with single-agent systems, this commitment expresses a promise and has some measure of persistence to future conduct, but the commitment is made between two agents and therefore it is a *mutual promise* to the later conduct of the agents involved. Hence, in addition to individual commitments, the theory developed in this work attempts to define and formalise agent to agent commitments and the conditions that lead to their formation and maintenance.

Based on this theory, a set of rules are developed which specify under what conditions various commitments are formed and under what conditions an agent needs to communicate certain facts, to which agent, and what it should communicate to that agent. By formally characterising these conditions, the rules specify the transition from a state in which such conditions hold, to a next valid state in which a commitment or a goal to communicate is formed. This way, the rules specify the reasoning process of an agent in relation to its interactions to other agents. The link between the theory and the modelling of the reasoning processes during the design and implementation phases, is in essence these specification rules.

In the design and implementation phase, to model the reasoning about interactions, we need a model of reasoning about actions in general, and for this we require a complete model of an agent in order to ensure the required input to the reasoning process and observe the effect of this process on the agent's behaviour in its environment and with the other agents. This task in its entirety is highly complex and beyond the scope of this book. Therefore, the reasoning about interactions is modelled in the (extended) COSY (COoperating Systems) agent architecture [BS92] whose underlying principles supports the BDI-concept. The original model consisted of a relatively simple reasoning mechanism for selecting actions. Based on the theory developed in this book, this mechanism is extended in order to permit reasoning and decisions about interactions in general, and modified by explicitly representing beliefs, desires and intentions and reasoning about actions in terms of the interplay of these attitudes. Having this general reasoning mechanism, it is illustrated how the specification of the reasoning about interactions in relation to task delegation and task adoption may be modelled in such an agent architecture.

One issue worth mentioning here is that as stated earlier the material presented in this book brings together many important topics in agent oriented technology which are also of interest to the studies related to the *Agent Oriented Programming* (AOP) paradigm [Sho93]. But since executional issues are not addressed in this book, the question of whether the specification rules presented in the approach may be directly executed, compiled, or simply used as abstract guidelines, are left open.

1.4.3 Outline of this Book

The book is structured as follows: Chapter 2 provides a literature survey of the philosophical and theoretical approaches to intentional systems. Chapter 3 presents the logical framework developed and describes the theory of commitments. Chapter 4 provides the specification of formation of commitments and the formation of goals to communicate in attempt to arrive at an agreement to cooperate. Chapter 5 describes the COSY agent architecture and discusses the extension and the modifications incurred, and furthermore describes how the specification of reasoning about interactions may be modelled in this architecture. Finally chapter 6 provides a summary, conclusion, evaluation and links to possible future research directions.

2. Review of the Theories on Agents as Intentional Systems

2.1 Overview

Motivated by Dennett's philosophy of *ladder of personhood* described in the previous chapter, this chapter first describes the formal theories related to *intentional systems*. The first section (Section 2.2) will provide a brief summary of various approaches to formalising intentional attitudes. Given this background, Section 2.3 will provide a survey of formalisms on knowledge and belief (i.e., informational attitudes), and Section 2.4 outlines some of the related theories that have aimed to capture the characteristic properties of motivational attitudes such as intentions, desires, and preferences. Section 2.6 will then extend the notion of intentional systems to issues related to reciprocity, and provide the related formalisms that have aimed to model joint attitudes of a group of agents, such as their mutual belief, joint goals and joint intentions. In order to arrive at such joint intentional status, agents may need to reason about when, how and what to communicate to their interacting partners. Therefore, Section 2.7 will provide the survey of material related to communication in multi-agent systems, and finally, Section 2.8 will conclude this chapter.

2.2 Formal Approaches to Intentional Attitudes

In developing formalisms, there are two problems to be addressed: the language of formulation and the semantic model [Kon86a]. Intentional notions are most commonly formulated by using a *modal logic* or some variations of it. In brief, the syntax of a modal language is that of classical languages (propositional or first-order) with addition of non-truth-functional modal operators. Many however believe that anything that can be represented in non-classical languages such as modal logic, can be reduced to a problem in first-order logic. Hence they propose that intentional notions such as beliefs, desires and so forth, can be represented and reasoned about in first-order *meta-level* languages [Moo85], [Mor86]. A meta-language is a many sorted first-order language containing terms which denote formulae of some other object language. Hence function and predicate terms may be first-order formulae of some other language. Reichgelt [Rei89] observes however that translation of modal languages to first-order meta languages is complicated and non-intuitive and furthermore, theorem proving is very inefficient. In practice therefore meta-languages seem to offer no great advantages over normal modal logic.

Two traditions to semantic modelling of intentional notions are the *possible world semantics* [Hin62] and the *sentential* or *interpreted symbolic structure* [Kon86a]. In the former approach, the truth value of beliefs is evaluated using an accessibility relation between *possible worlds*. In the sentential approach beliefs are viewed as symbolic formulae explicitly represented in a data structure associated with a system. For the remainder of this book we will be mainly concerned with modal logic and possible world semantics and some variations of it and refer the reader to [Kon86a] for more discussions on various syntax and semantics employed to represent and reason about intentional notions.

2.3 Knowledge and Belief

A widely acknowledged work on the logic of knowledge and belief (known as *epistemic logic* or to be precise, *doxastic logic*) dates back to the work of Hintikka in 1962 [Hin62]. It was found that classical logics in their standard form were not appropriate for reasoning about intentional notions. As Wooldridge [Woo92] states:

> "The problem is that intentional notions – such as beliefs and desires – are referentially opaque, in that they set up opaque contexts in which the standard substitution rules of first-order logic do not apply. In classical (propositional and first-order) logic, the denotation, or semantic value, of an expression is dependent solely on the denotations of its sub-expressions. For example, the denotation of the propositional logic formula $p \wedge q$ is a function of the truth-values of p and q. In contrast, the intentional notions are <u>not</u> truth functional. It is surely not the case that the truth-value of the sentence: "Janine believes p" is dependent solely on the truth-value of p."

Hintikka introduced the idea of applying the *possible worlds semantics* to intentional notions, using the Kripke structure [Kri63] as his logical tool. He first set out the approach in terms of a set of sentences called *model sets* and an *alternativeness relation* between the model sets [Hin62]. Later, he recast the approach in terms of the now standard notions of possible worlds and *accessibility* relations between the *possible worlds* [Hin72] (c.f. [McA88]). The main idea is that there is a set of worlds that an agent considers possible, as given by the accessibility relation. The concept of possible worlds is not at all a clear one, but the following example may help us to have a grasp of it:

As an example, suppose Anna was in a workshop where she meets José who comes from Mexico. Later she decides to contact him but she realises that she never registered his surname in mind and also does not know which institute he is associated with. In searching through the list of affiliations provided in the workshop, she finds two people with the name José, incidentally both coming from Mexico! Given what Anna knows (with no further information), therefore, the only possible affiliations are these two, each considered as a *world* [1] or *state of affairs*. Anything that is true in all the worlds is said to be believed. For instance, in this example, Anna believes 'José comes from Mexico'.

The language of possible world semantics is a normal modal logic. Modal logic was originally developed to formalise arguments involving the notions of *necessity* and *possibility*. A necessary proposition is a *true* proposition which could not be *false*, on the other hand a possible proposition is one which may happen to be *true*. With respect to the concept of possible worlds, then, a necessary proposition is the one which is true in all worlds, and a possible proposition is the one that is true at least in one world. In the above example, 'José lives in Mexico' is a necessary proposition while each of the two affiliations is a possible affiliation of the José in question.

The syntax of modal logic is that of classical logic, with the addition of two modal operators: $\Box$ (necessity), and $\Diamond$ (possibility). The possibility operator may also be defined in terms of the necessity operator: $\Diamond\varphi \stackrel{def}{=} \neg\Box\neg\varphi$.

The semantics are defined in terms of a *model* or a *frame* $M = \langle W, R, \pi \rangle$, where:

(i) W is a set of possible worlds;
(ii) R is a binary relation on W, called the *accessibility relation*;
(iii) π is an *assignment function* which determines for each world $w \in W$, the truth values of the atomic propositions in w.

Formulae are then interpreted according to a pair $\langle M, w \rangle$, (for some world w, $w \in W$), using the *satisfaction relation* ('$\models$') as shown in Figure 2.1. A formula is said to be *satisfiable* if it is satisfied in at least one model/world pair, and said to be *valid* if it is true in every model/world pair.

$$
\begin{array}{lll}
\langle M, w \rangle & \models & \text{true} \\
\langle M, w \rangle & \models & p & \text{where } p \in Prop, \text{ iff } p \in \pi(w) \\
\langle M, w \rangle & \models & \neg\varphi & \text{iff } \langle M, w \rangle \not\models \varphi \\
\langle M, w \rangle & \models & \varphi \vee \psi & \text{iff } \langle M, w \rangle \models \varphi \text{ or } \langle M, w \rangle \models \psi \\
\langle M, w \rangle & \models & \Box\varphi & \text{iff } \forall w' \in W . \text{ if } (w, w') \in R \text{ then } \langle M, w' \rangle \models \varphi \\
\langle M, w \rangle & \models & \Diamond\varphi & \text{iff } \exists w' \in W . (w, w') \in R \text{ and } \langle M, w' \rangle \models \varphi
\end{array}
$$

Fig. 2.1. Semantics of Propositional Modal Logic

---

[1] Hintikka refers to these worlds as *epistemic alternatives*.

Some of the well-known properties of modal propositional logic are listed below [Che80]:

K: $\models \Box(\varphi \Rightarrow \psi) \Rightarrow (\Box\varphi \Rightarrow \Box\psi)$

T: $\Box\varphi \Rightarrow \varphi$

D: $\Box\varphi \Rightarrow \Diamond\varphi$, or alternatively, $\Box\varphi \Rightarrow \neg\Box\neg\varphi$

4: $\Box\varphi \Rightarrow \Box\Box\varphi$

5: $\Diamond\varphi \Rightarrow \Box\Diamond\varphi$, or alternatively, $\neg\Box\neg\varphi \Rightarrow \Box\neg\Box\neg\varphi$

NEC: if $\models \varphi$ then $\Box\varphi$

The K axiom is valid and therefore is a theorem of any axiomatisation of normal modal logic. The other axioms correspond to the properties of the accessibility relation R. For instance axiom T is true in a class of models where R is reflexive. This correspondence is represented in the left two columns of table 2.1. The last property (R1) is known as the *rule of necessitation* (NEC) which is an inference rule in any axiomatisation of normal modal logic.

Table 2.1. Axioms and Systems of Normal Modal Logic

Axioms	*Property of R*	Systems	Axiomatisations
T	reflexive	**T**	KT
D	serial	**S4**	KD4
4	transitive	**weak-S5**	KD45
5	Euclidean	**S5**	KT5

It can immediately be observed that by imposing various restrictions on the accessibility relation, we obtain different *systems* of modal propositional logic, where a system of logic is a set of formulae valid in some class of models and each member of the set is called a *theorem*. As was noted before, K is a theorem in any axiomatisation of modal logic and therefore is true in any system. The systems of interest to the study of epistemic logic have been the systems T, $S4$, *weak-S5* and $S5$ corresponding to the axiomatisations presented in the rightmost column of table 2.1.

Epistemic logic was developed by replacing the necessity operator ($\Box$) with the (K) operator for *knowledge*. In single agent systems, $K\varphi$ means that 'the agent knows φ'. To account for multi-agent settings, a subscript may be added to the operator to denote a specific agent in the setting. So for instance, 'K_i' denotes that 'agent i knows that φ'. And its semantics is defined as follows:

$$\langle M, w \rangle \models K_i\varphi \text{ iff } \forall w' \in W \text{ . if } (w, w') \in R_i \text{ then } \langle M, w' \rangle \models \varphi$$

With respect to epistemic logic the above axioms and the rule of necessitation are interpreted as follows:

K: An agent's knowledge is closed under implication, that is, it knows all the consequences of its beliefs.

T: This axiom is known as the *knowledge axiom* since it implies what an agent knows is thereby 'true'. knows everything that holds.

D: An agent's beliefs are non-contradictory, that is, if it believes some proposition holds, then it does not believe in the negation of that proposition simultaneously.

4: This axiom is known as *positive introspection* and denotes that an agent knows 'what it knows'.

5: This axiom is known as *negative introspection* and similarly denotes that an agent knows 'what it does not know'.

NEC: The rule of necessitation dictates that an agent knows every valid formulae and therefore also all the tautologies.

Knowledge may be distinguished from belief by considering knowledge as being true belief: $K_i\varphi \Leftrightarrow B_i\varphi \wedge \varphi$.

Logical Omniscience

The necessitation rule and the K axiom together mean that an agent believes all valid formulae and knows all the logical consequences of its beliefs. This is known as the *logical omniscience* [Hin62]. The resulting consequences of logical omniscience are known as:

Logical consistency, which says that an agent should not believe in φ and ψ simultaneously, if $\varphi \Rightarrow \neg\psi$. Humans, however, often believe in φ and ψ simultaneously without being aware of implicit inconsistency that results from $\varphi \Rightarrow \neg\psi$. Whether human or machine, an agent is resource bounded, (i.e., bounded in terms of the computational time and space in memory that it consumes). Clearly so, knowing the consequences of one's beliefs and consequently being (logically) consistent, seems to be too large a demand to be imposed on computationally limited agents [Kon86a].

Logical equivalence, which says that given two propositions (i) φ, and (ii) $\varphi \wedge \psi$, where ψ is valid, (i) and (ii) are logically equivalent. While if ψ is valid, it is therefore believed, the possible world semantics would have us commit to the fact that logical equivalent propositions are equivalent as beliefs (see [Kon86a]).

To avoid the problem of logical omniscience a number of approaches have been proposed which will be discussed later. Wooldridge summarises the problems associates with normal modal logic as a logic of knowledge and belief as follows ([Woo92], page 24-25):

– agents believe all valid formulae;
– agents' beliefs are closed under logical consequence;
– equivalent propositions are identical beliefs;

- if agents are inconsistent, then they believe everything;
- in the worst case automation is not feasible;

The last point refers to the findings of Halpern and Moses who examined the computational and proof-theoretic properties of normal modal logic [HM92]. They concluded that although the provability of these systems are decidable, the satisfiability and validity problems are PSPACE complete. Therefore, in the worse case, automation is not a possibility.

Despite these disadvantages, possible world semantics has been commonly used by the practitioners and still appears to be the most appropriate model for describing and reasoning about belief and knowledge.

Nevertheless, it is worth mentioning a few words on some of the alternative approaches for formalising and reasoning about belief. A commonly known alternative is the *syntactic approach*, in which what an agent knows is explicitly represented by a set of formulae in its knowledge base [Ebe74]. Since the approach does not consider models of the world, this set need not be constrained to be closed under logical consequence or to contain all instances of a given axiom scheme. But for the same reason, it does not assign semantic content to knowledge and as a result it is extensively difficult to analyse. *"If knowledge is represented by an arbitrary set of formulae, we have no principles to guide a KB analysis"* [Hal86]. The sentential approach is somewhat more sophisticated than the syntactic approach, in that explicit beliefs are the primary beliefs and implicit beliefs are derived from them by closure under logical consequence. Konolige states that generally in giving a formal characterisation of explicit beliefs, one attempts to capture how agents syntactically derive one belief from others. One example of such a system is Konolige's *deduction model* [Kon86a] which is based on the observation that AI knowledge bases usually consist of a core set of basic beliefs and a deductive mechanism for deriving some, but not all, logical consequences of the core set. But he also argues that the sentential approach will only work under certain circumstances.

Alternative approaches exist which attempt to avoid the problem of logical omniscience by mixing the sentential and possible worlds approaches. One such scheme is due to Levesque [Lev84], who also distinguishes between *implicit* and *explicit* beliefs. The value of beliefs are evaluated in *situations* rather than worlds. A situation can be thought as a fragment of a world or a partial description of a world. In contrast to the possible world model, where propositions may be assigned either of true or false, in a situation, a proposition may be assigned one of: true, false, none or both. Consequently, since propositions are not truth-functional, the necessitation rule (i.e., knowing all the valid formulae) does not pose any problem. Also in Levesque's approach, explicit belief is not closed under logical consequence and an agent can be inconsistent without believing everything. Although this approach is claimed to solve the problem of logical omniscience, it does not allow quantification[2], meta-reasoning (i.e., an agent reasoning about its own knowledge) and reasoning about several agents.

In criticising Levesque's approach, Fagin and Halpern [FH85] have shown that under certain circumstances, an agent modelled by this scheme must still be aware of propositional tautologies (c.f. [Woo92]). To overcome this problem, they set out an alternative approach known as *logic of general awareness*. In this approach explicit beliefs are derived from what an agent is aware of and what is true in all its epistemic worlds, i.e., what it implicitly believes. As a result, an agent can distinguish between what it is actually aware of and what it knows nothing about. In examining this approach, Konolige [Kon86b] argues that as far as resource bounded reasoning from beliefs is concerned, there is not much to be gained by the logic of general awareness, it is no more powerful than the deduction model, and can be re-expressed in those terms. Furthermore, like other approaches (e.g., [Ash86] and [SA92]) which seek to avoid the logical omniscience problem by mixing the sentential and possible worlds semantics, the logic of general awareness is technically more complex than either of semantic models.

2.4 Intentions

Apart from knowledge and belief, other mental attitudes contributing to the rational behaviour of an agent are intentions, desires, preferences and the like. Bratman [Bra90] calls these *pro-attitudes* and distinguishes them from knowledge and belief in that pro-attitudes in their general sense play a *motivational* role and it is in concert with beliefs that they can move us to act. He further distinguishes pro-attitudes such as desires and preferences as being *potential influencers of conduct* (in general), from intentions which are *conduct-controllers*.

In the philosophical literature, intentions have been studied along seemingly different dimensions. Although the distinctions between these dimensions are not always entirely obvious, their explanation may help us make clear in what sense intentions are used in the context of designing intentional systems. Bratman distinguishes *future-directed* intentions from *present-directed* intentions[3]. Future-directed intention (or according to Searle [Sea83] *prior* intention) is the intention to achieve a particular future state of the world. It is basically in this sense that intentions are said to be useful in the context of rational intelligent agents. Present-directed intentions are said to be mainly of interest to philosophers whose primary concern is to differentiate intended behaviours from unintended behaviours such as reflexes.

---

[2] Levesque's approach was however extended by Patel-Schneider [PS85] and Lakemeyer [Lak86] who provide a semantics for a first-order logic of knowledge.

[3] Brand [Bra84] uses the terms *prospective* and *immediate* intentions

Another dimension of analysis is between *intending something* (or *intention to act*), and *doing intentionally*. The former refers to the conditions that are actually intended by the agent to bring about, whereas the latter stresses the action that the agent (intentionally) chooses to perform. For example, suppose I intend to open a locked door, to do so, I (intentionally) choose to turn the key clockwise believing that this is the common rotating direction to unlock. As it occurs, after I have performed my intended action, I realise that I have actually double locked the door since the lock that I am dealing with is setup differently. Therefore I may choose to perform an action and believing (with high expectations) that this action would bring about my intended condition, but it may occur that my intentionally chosen action fails to bring about my intended condition. A derivative and somewhat delicate difference here is that, an agent may not always explicitly intend (in the sense of prior intentions) the conditions that result successfully from its (intentionally) chosen actions. For instance my moving the arm, holding, inserting and rotating the key and all the inter-relationships between my physical movements and the resulting actions and conditions are not thought out *a priori* when I intended to unlock the door.

Many argue that present-directed intentions and 'doing intentionally' are basically more useful in explanation and prediction. Singh [Sin95] for example, states that analysis of intentions in this form to distinguish which behaviour is intended and which is not, does not seem to bear much importance in computer science. As far as design of artificial agents is concerned, the behaviours that an agent may perform, be it actions that are intended or reflexes, can be regarded as actions that are done as part of some prior intentions. In view of this book however, both types of intentions are important for the design of artificial systems, not necessarily to distinguish actions from reflexes, but to distinguish the *intended ends* from the *intended means*.

Many philosophers believe that intentions to act (prior intentions) are reducible to certain desires and beliefs and do not have a distinct role in the mental life of rational agents. Bratman argues otherwise and sets out to describe the functional role or characteristic of intentions by sketching the relation between beliefs, desires, intentions, perception, action and cognitive activities such as practical reasoning. He brings our attention to two contrasting literatures on practical reasoning. First is the field of decision theory where:

> "... *Practical reasoning is a matter of weighing conflicting considerations for and against conflicting options, where the relevant considerations are provided by what the agent desires/values/cares about and what the agent believes. Practical reasoning consists in weighing desire-belief reasons for and against conflicting courses of action. ... what is important to notice about this model of practical reasoning is that it provides no distinctive role for an agent's future-directed intentions as inputs to such reasoning.*" ([Bra90], page 17)

In contrast, in view of the "planning problem", practical reasoning is reasoning from prior intentions and relevant beliefs to derivative intentions concerning means, preliminary steps, or more specific courses of action. Bratman notes that the two are related and the key is the role of intentions as input to further reasoning.

> "*My intention today to go to Monterey tomorrow helps coordinate my activities for this week, and my activities with yours, by entering into a larger plan of action—one that will eventually include specifications of how to get there and what to bring, and one that will be coordinated with, for example, my child-care plans and your plans for meeting me in Monterey. And it will do this in ways compatible with my resource limitations and in a way that extends the influence of today's deliberation to tomorrow's action*" ([Bra90], page 18)

The important property of intentions is that they involve a measure of commitment to action and endeavouring to bring about the intended ends. Such a commitment shapes an agent's later conduct and enables intra- and interpersonal coordination. To serve this purpose well, once an intention is adopted an agent must find the means of satisfying it by filling in the appropriate plans with subplans and means of fulfilling the subplans. Bratman calls this *means-end analysis*. A derivative requirement here is tracking the success or failure of existing intentions in order to replan, should an existing plan fail to meet its intended ends. It is due to these properties (i.e., that the intentions move an agent to do some means-end analysis and replan if required), that Bratman notes: "*intentions frequently pose problems for future deliberation*".

The next requirement is that intentions must be mutually consistent, that is, an agent should not commit itself to options that are in conflict with its existing intentions. Such inconsistencies would make the mental state too incoherent for an agent to act [Sin95]. Hence intentions provide a *filter of admissibility* [BIP88][Bra90], meaning that they constrain further intentions and limit the number of options to be considered for deliberation. Bratman states that all this requires prior intentions and plans to have certain stability. Prior intentions and plans resist being reconsidered or abandoned, but it would be also irrational to treat one's prior plans as irrevocable.

This has motivated several lines of research towards the study of the policies governing reconsideration of intentions and the measure of commitment considered as rational for resource-bounded limited agents. This is one of the topics that will be covered later in this section and further in chapter 3.

Relationship between Beliefs and Intentions

The relationship between belief and intention is outlined below which will be served as a reference for the future sections that follow.

1. *Intention-belief consistency:* In giving an account of the relationship between beliefs and intentions, Bratman notes that "*there is a defeasible*

demand that one's intentions be consistent with one's beliefs", that is, an agent (i) should believe that its intended objective is possible, (ii) does not believe that it will not reach its objective, and (iii) given the right conditions believe that it will achieve its objective.

2. *Intention-belief incompleteness:* While intentions must be consistent with an agents beliefs, they should not necessarily entail beliefs. That is, an agent intending a condition should not necessarily believe that the condition <u>will</u> be eventually true. In other words, it is perfectly rational of an agent to have incomplete beliefs about her intentions.

Bratman refers to these two principles (i.e., *intention-belief consistency* and *intention-belief incompleteness*) as the *asymmetry thesis* [RG91a].

3. *Side-effect problem:* A related topic regarding the relation between beliefs and intentions which has received considerable attention in the literature is the so-called *side-effect problem* [Bra87], [CL90], [RG91a]. Bratman uses an example of a strategic bomber who intends to bomb a munition factory and also believes that doing so would kill all the children in the nearby school. Using this example, he argues: "*an agent who intends to do α and believes that doing α would require it to do β does not have to also intend β*".

Relationship between Desires and Intentions

It is the set of properties associated with intentions discussed so far, that distinguishes intentions from desires. Following summarises these distinctions:

1. *Internal consistency:* While an agent should avoid conflicting intentions, it may have conflicting desires. For example, one may have both the desire of having an old Mercedes car and saving on petrol.

2. *Means-end analysis:* Intentions pose problems for future deliberation. With desires this may not be necessarily so. For example I may have a desire of going on a cruise round the world, but never really set out to do so.

3. *Tracking success and failures:* As with the previous property– tracking the success or failure of intentions and replanning in case of failures–, relies on the important property of intentions (i.e., commitment to action and endeavouring to bring about the intended ends). With desires *per se* there is no commitment associated. In this view, intentions may be said to be desires plus commitment to act and fulfill them.

4. *Consistency with belief:* Intentions should be consistent with beliefs, that is, one does not intend something that one does not believe to be possible. With desires however this may not necessarily hold.

So due to Bratman, while desires and other attitudes are *influencers of conduct*, intentions are *conduct-controllers*. For example, my desire to go to the movies tonight <u>may</u> influence what I would plan for tonight, whereas, once I have the intention of going to the movies tonight, the matter is settled I

believe that I will go and this belief and the related commitment <u>will</u> shape
my other activities for tonight.

2.4.1 Cohen and Levesque's Formalism

The notion of intention has initially found its way in AI in the field of
speech act theory to aid dialogue planning and interpretation, see for example [CP79], [AP80], [App85]. The first formalisation of intentions was due
to Allen [All84] in who's view intentions are reducible to beliefs about future
actions. This however proves to be problematic since as was described earlier
intentions have a distinct role that distinguishes them from beliefs. Allen's
work in any case was indirectly aimed at formalising and analysing intentions. The first direct attempt to provide a logical analysis of the concept
was made by Cohen and Levesque[4] [CL86], [CL90], who also required it in
order to develop a theory of speech acts. Following Bratman's philosophical
work C&L set out to specify the *"rational balance"* among beliefs, goals, intentions, commitments and actions of autonomous agents, and explore the
relationship that intention plays in maintaining the balance.

This original work has set the grounds for many formalisms that have since
been developed for reasoning about various properties of agents. Therefore,
it is worthwhile to give a more detailed account of this work.

The Logical Framework

The language of formulation is a many-sorted, first-order, multi-modal logic
with equality. Apart from usual operators of first-order logic, it consists of
four primitive modal operators, namely, *Happens, Done,* BEL and GOAL.
The semantics of these constructs are given using possible-world semantics.
The world is defined as a discrete sequence of events, temporally extended
infinitely into past and future. The two basic temporal operators, *Happens*
and *Done* respectively define a sequence of events that happen next, and a
sequence of events that have just happened. Complex actions are constructed
using operators similar to those in dynamic logic [Har79]: '$e; e'$' (e followed
by e'), '$e|e'$' (e or e'), '$e?$' (test action), and '$e*$' (iterative action).

The temporal operators: "$\Box$" (always), "$\Diamond$" (eventually)[5], LATER and
BEFORE[6] are then defined in terms of happening of events over a linear time
space with their intuitive meaning.

The semantics of BEL and GOAL is given by belief- and goal-accessibility
relations on possible worlds. It is assumed that an agent's goal-accessibility

---

[4] Henceforth, C&L.

[5] These operators should not be mistaken with the *"necessity"* and *"possibility"*
operators of normal modal logic.

[6] (BEFORE φ ψ) is a temporal precedence operator which holds, if φ holds before
ψ.

relation is a subset of its belief-accessibility relation. This is called the *realism constraint*. This constraint is meant to ensure that the worlds chosen by an agent are not ruled out by his beliefs. One important property which results from this assumption is the following proposition:

CL 1. $\models$ (BEL $x\ \varphi$) $\Rightarrow$ (GOAL $x\ \varphi$).

That is, *"if an agent believes that φ is true now, he cannot now want it to be currently false, agents cannot choose what they cannot change"*[CL90]. This proposition however, leads to other problems which will be discussed later.

They first set out to define achievement goals as goals that are currently false and the agent desires to bring about later.

CL 2. Achievement Goal

$$(\text{A\_GOAL } x\ \varphi) \overset{def}{=} (\text{GOAL } x\ (\text{LATER } \varphi)) \land (\text{BEL } x\ \neg\varphi).$$

Following this definition, they provide the assumption that agents do not persist forever on a goal, and will eventually drop it:

CL 3. $\models \Diamond\neg$(GOAL x (LATER φ)).

They then go on to define *persistent goals*, in order to capture the conditions required in order to remain committed to a goal and the conditions that should hold before the goal is dropped. For this, they identify two main strategies: (i) *strong persistent goal*, which requires an agent to drop a goal if either it is achieved, or it will never be achieved; and (ii) *relativised persistent goal*, that is defined relative to a condition that originally led to adopting the goal (i.e., the motivation). In this case in addition to the above conditions, an agent would drop a goal if the original motivation no longer exists. The latter is formally defined as shown below:

CL 4. Relativised Persistent Goal
$$(\text{P\_R\_GOAL } x\ \varphi\ q) \overset{def}{=} (\text{A\_GOAL } x\ \varphi) \land$$
$$(\text{BEFORE } [(\text{BEL } x\ \varphi) \lor (\text{BEL } x\ \Box\ \neg\varphi) \lor (\text{BEL } x\ \neg q)]$$
$$(\neg(\text{GOAL } x\ (\text{LATER } \varphi)))).$$

They then define two types of intentions: (a) intention to act, and (b) intend to bring about a state of affairs. Intention to act (INTEND$_1$) is defined as a persistent, relativised goal to *"have done"* an action α, as demonstrated below:

CL 5. Intention to act
$$(\text{INTEND}_1\ x\ \alpha\ \psi) \overset{def}{=}$$
$$(\text{P\_R\_GOAL } x\ [(Done\ x\ (\text{BEL } x\ (Happens\ x\ \alpha; \varphi?)))?; \alpha; \varphi?)]\ \psi).$$

They argue that defining intention in terms of persistent goal of *"to have done α"*, (as opposed to a commitment *"to do α"*), avoids the agent to be committed to doing something accidentally or unknowingly. With regards to Bratman's future-directed intentions, they state:

"It seems reasonable to require that the agent be committed to believing he is about to do the intended action, and then doing it. Thus, intentions are future-directed, but here directed towards something happening next. This is as close one can come to present directed intention."

They then define intention to bring about a state of affairs (INTEND$_2$) as follows:

CL 6. Intention to achieve a state of affairs

$$(\text{INTEND}_2 \; x \; \varphi \; \psi) \stackrel{def}{=} (\text{P\_R\_GOAL} \; x \; \exists e \; (Done \; x \; p?; e; \varphi?) \; \psi).$$

where
$$p \stackrel{def}{=} \left[\begin{array}{l} (\text{BEL} \; x \; \exists e' \; (Happens \; x \; e'; \varphi?)) \; \wedge \\ \neg(\text{GOAL} \; x \; \neg(Happens \; x \; e; \varphi?)) \end{array} \right].$$

They explain the definition in a number of steps:

1. To intend to bring about φ, an agent is committed to doing some sequence of events e himself, after which φ holds[7];
2. Prior to doing e to bring about φ, (i.e., the conjunctions within square braces):
   (a) The agent believes that it is *about to do something* (event sequence e') bringing about φ[8]; and
   (b) the agent does not have as a goal e's not bringing about φ[9].

The authors state that with respect to the first conjunct (i.e., part (a)), an agent would require to have a plan for bringing it about, which is very difficult to define.

Criticisms of Cohen and Levesque's Formalism

Cohen and Levesque emphasise that the formalism should be regarded as a description or specification *of* an agent, rather than one that any agent could or should use to reason. Unhappy with this account, Sadek criticises C&L's approach in that:

"...[the approach] does not account for subjective point of view and is often of an a posteriori nature. ... With this approach, one cannot say whether, at a given moment, an agent actually has some given mental attitude; one can only say whether the agent has behaved as if she has some given mental attitudes. Hence, the resulting theory does not necessarily characterise introspective agents; so it cannot be straightforwardly embedded in the operational model of an autonomous agent." ([Sad92], page 463)

---

[7] (P_R_GOAL x $\exists e$ (*Done x* ([...]?; e; φ?) ψ).
[8] (BEL x $\exists e'$ (*Happens x e'; φ?*))
[9] ($\neg$GOAL x $\neg$(*Happens x e; φ?*))

Further, as opposed to the title of their work (i.e., intention *is* choice with commitment), the theory does not explicitly capture the notion of 'choice'. This is as a consequence of the characterisation of achievement goals (CL2) according to which, "whenever an agent believes that a property is false yet possible, she is considered as having this property as an achievement goal" (c.f. [Sad92], page 462). Rao and Georgeff show that this is essentially the problem due to the realism constraint (i.e., $\mathcal{G} \subseteq \mathcal{B}$) [RG91a]. They state that although this constraint captures some aspects of Bratman's *asymmetry thesis*, it is unsatisfactory in that any beliefs about the future thereby become adopted as goals. Furthermore, it leads to certain problems concerning the side-effects of actions.

Another critic of C&L's theory is Singh whose criticism is directed more to the conceptual and technical aspects of the theory than its operationality.

> "*The nesting of definitions makes Cohen and Levesque's theory the most complicated of the works on intentions. Their theory also suffers from several conceptual and technical shortcomings. Their definition confuses the semantics of intentions with constraints on intention revision. ...A technical shortcoming is that certain properties are stated as "easy to see," but it is possible to construct counterexamples to these properties in the theory itself.*" ([Sin95], chapter 3.5)

Singh's thorough examination of C&L's theory and the related criticisms can be found in [Sin92], a short account of which is outlined below:

- One problem originates from the assumption CL3 that states, agents eventually drop their goals. The assumption does not involve actions and *abilities* of an agent in any way. As a result the policies for goal revision (i.e., P_GOAL and P_R_GOAL) do not address three important properties: (i) ability of an agent to act, (ii) that the agent actually acts for the goal, and (iii) success or failure of an action. Since intentions are a special kind of persistent goals, (given the shortcomings of the definitions for persistent goals), they do not necessarily *move an agent to act*, which is obviously counterintuitive to the whole concept of the theory.
- A restrictive feature of the theory is that only one event can occur at a time. Given the definition of intentions (CL5 and CL6), agents can have no more than one intention at any time that they can act on. This yields two problems: (i) in reality this is not the case, and (ii) actions of other agents cannot be taken into account, and therefore the theory does not allow different agents to act in an interleaved manner.
- Since the theory does not capture the essential distinction between the semantics of intentions and policies of when and when not to update them, it prevents us from stating that an agent intends something *simpliciter* : we have to state in advance the conditions under which a given intention may be given up. If these conditions are specified nonmonotonically, the

semantics of intentions depends on an *ad hoc* manner of how an agent deliberates about his beliefs and intentions.

2.4.2 Rao and Georgeff's Formalism

Inspired by the work of C&L and following the philosophical work of Bratman, Rao and Georgeff[10] [RG91c] developed their own formalism for modelling rational agents. This formalism also sets the foundation of the theory of commitments in the next chapter, and therefore will be described in greater detail in Section 3.3.4.

Their formalism extends CTL* (Computational Tree Logic) [Eme90] - a propositional branching-time temporal logic - to first-order logic with addition of modalities for belief, goal and intention.

The world is modelled using a temporal structure with a branching time future and a single past, called a *time-tree*. A particular time point in a particular world is called a *situation*. Situations are mapped to one another by occurrence of events. The branches in a time-tree can be viewed as representing the *choices* available to the agent at each moment in time.

There are two path operators 'E' (optional) and 'A' (inevitable). A path formula ψ is said to be optional if at a particular point in a time-tree, ψ is true of at least one path emanating from that point; and it is said to be inevitable if ψ is true on all paths emanating from that point. The standard temporal operators $\Diamond$ (eventually), $\Box$ (always), $\bigcirc$ (next) and $\mathcal{U}$ (until), operate over state and path formulae. These modalities can be combined in various ways to describe the options of an agent.

Beliefs, goals and intentions are modelled as a set of belief-, goal- and intention-accessible worlds associated to an agent in each situation. Multiple worlds result from an agent's lack of knowledge about the states of the world. But within each of these worlds, the branching future represents the choice (option) still available to the agent in selecting which action to perform. An agent is said to have a belief φ, at time point t, if and only if φ is true in all its belief-accessible worlds. Similarly for goals and intentions.

They distinguish between goals and desires in that: (i) while desires can be inconsistent with one another, the goals must be consistent. In other words, goals are chosen desires of the agent that are consistent; and (ii) the agent should believe that the goal is achievable (this is called *belief-goal compatibility*). This last property corresponds to C&L's *realism* constraint, and will be discussed later.

The relationship between belief, goal and intention is stated as follows: An agent moves from a belief-accessible world to a desire-accessible world by *desiring* future paths, and from a desire-accessible world to an intention-accessible world by *committing* to certain desired future paths.

---

[10] Henceforth, R&G.

Realism and Strong Realism Constraints

According to C&L's formalism goal-accessibility worlds are a subset of belief-accessibility worlds, (i.e. $\mathcal{G} \subseteq \mathcal{B}$). As each possible world in their formalism is a time-line, this imposes the condition that the chosen (or desire-accessible) worlds be compatible with the agent's belief-accessible worlds. In other words, (BEL $x\ \varphi$) $\Rightarrow$ (GOAL $x\ \varphi$). Although, this axiom ensures that goals of an agent are not ruled out by its beliefs, it also forces the agent to adopt as goals certain inevitable facts about the world [RG91a]. R&G instead introduce the notion of *strong realism* which is captured by imposing the following restrictions:

1. $\forall w' \in \mathcal{B}_t^w\ \exists w'' \in \mathcal{G}_t^w$ such that $w'' \sqsubseteq w'$.
2. $\forall w' \in \mathcal{G}_t^w\ \exists w'' \in \mathcal{I}_t^w$ such that $w'' \sqsubseteq w'$.

The first constraint means that for every belief-accessible world w at time-point t, there is a desire-accessible world w' at that time-point which is sub-world of w. But the converse does not necessarily hold, i.e., there can be desire-accessible worlds that do not have corresponding belief-accessible worlds. The second constraint expresses a similar constraint, but between goal- and intention-accessible worlds. Following the belief-goal and goal-intention compatibility constraints, the following axioms are given for O-formulae[11]:

RG 1. (GOAL $x\ \varphi$) $\Rightarrow$ (BEL $x\ \varphi$).

RG 2. (INTEND $x\ \varphi$) $\Rightarrow$ (GOAL $x\ \varphi$).

Supposing φ is $E\psi$, the first axiom above states that if agent x has the goal that ψ is optionally true, she also believes it, that is, there is at least one path in all the belief-accessible worlds in which ψ is true.

Belief-goal compatibility and goal-intention compatibility axioms together ensure Bratman's belief-intention consistency requirement. Hence the strong realism constraint along with the above axioms exhibits the following important features:

- Ensure that goals and intentions, while having to be consistent, need not be closed under the beliefs of the agent. Therefore, the formalism nicely captures Bratman's asymmetry thesis.
- Even if the agent believes that certain facts are inevitable, she is not forced to adopt them as goals (or as intentions). As a result, the side-effect problem is does not occur within this formalism.
- If an agent believes that a proposition is currently false but possible, the agent would not necessarily adopt it as a goal (or an intention). Therefore, it avoids the unwanted consequence of C&L's realism constraint.

---

[11] O-formula: contains no positive occurrences of inevitable outside the scope of modal operators BEL, GOAL or INTEND.

On top of these axioms, the authors provide axioms and the corresponding semantic conditions for *beliefs about intentions, beliefs about goals,* and *goals about intentions,* to express that intentions are stronger attitudes than goals and goals stronger than beliefs (see Section 3.3.4).

Axioms of Commitment

As with C&L, they also introduce an axiom in order to capture the requirement that intentions of an agent do not persist forever.

RG 3. (INTEND $x\ \varphi$) $\Rightarrow$ A $\Diamond\ \neg$(INTEND $x\ \varphi$).

They introduce three types of commitment strategies: *blind, single-minded* and *open-minded.* A blindly committed agent would maintain her intention to achieve φ until she believes that φ has been achieved. A single-minded agent maintains her intention as long as she believes that the intention is achievable, or believes that φ has been achieved. An open-minded agent maintains her intention to achieve φ as long as φ is still one of her goals. These are expressed in the following axioms:

RG 4. blind commitment

$$(\text{INTEND } x\ \text{A } \Diamond\ \varphi) \Rightarrow \text{A[(INTEND } x\ \text{A } \Diamond\ \varphi)\ \mathcal{U}\ (\text{BEL } x\ \varphi)].$$

RG 5. single-minded commitment

$$(\text{INTEND } x\ \text{A} \Diamond\ \varphi) \Rightarrow \text{A[(INTEND } x\ \text{A} \Diamond\ \varphi)\ \mathcal{U}\ (\text{BEL } x\ \varphi)\ \vee\ \neg(\text{BEL } x\ \text{E} \Diamond\ \varphi)].$$

RG 6. open-minded commitment

$$(\text{INTEND } x\ \text{A} \Diamond\ \varphi) \Rightarrow \text{A[(INTEND } x\ \text{A} \Diamond\ \varphi)\ \mathcal{U}\ (\text{BEL } x\ \varphi)\ \vee\ \neg(\text{GOAL } x\ \text{E} \Diamond\ \varphi)].$$

The authors however state that these are not the only possible commitment strategies. Furthermore, these strategies may be mixed, by for example, being open minded with respect to the ends but single-minded with respect to the means [RG91c].

One important and distinguishing part of this work as compared with C&L and many others' is the fact that the theory is not solely confined to the concepts of mental attitudes. In a follow up work [RGS92], they explicitly address the processes that lead to the formation of intentions. One of these is the *means-end reasoning* introduced by Bratman in [Bra90] (see Section 2.4), which involves reasoning about the means to achieve certain intended ends.

The formalism assumes a library of pre-compiled plans. Plans are syntactic structures with a precondition (*pre*(p)) and a body (*body*(p)). The body of a plan is a graph describing steps of the plan, each step may be an executable action or another (sub) goal. They model the means-end reasoning process of an agent in two ways ([RGS92], page 72). The first requirement is the minimal conditions that any rational agent needs to satisfy: (1)

> "... whenever an agent intends the body of a plan structure, then he
> must have a goal towards the purpose of the plan and the precondi-
> tions must be believed."

Formally:

$$\textbf{RG 7.} \models \frac{(Has\_plan\ x\ p\ \varphi) \wedge (\textsf{INTEND}\ x\ \langle body(p)\rangle) \Rightarrow}{(\textsf{GOAL}\ x\ \varphi) \wedge (\textsf{BEL}\ x\ \langle pre(p)\rangle)}$$

where $(Has\_plan\ x\ p\ \varphi)$, means that agent x has a plan p to achieve φ. They
argue however that this requirement is not sufficient for the agent to form
intentions and act based on these intentions. So they introduce additional
constraints for a strongly committed rational agent: (2)

> "If an individual agent has a plan p and has acquired the goal towards
> the purpose of this plan, and believes in the precondition of the plan,
> and it's deliberation function has chosen this plan, he will intend to
> execute the body of the plan."

Since the body of the plan may contain other achievement goals, by the
strong realism axiom, the agent would then be forced to adopt the resulting
sub-goals and intend the appropriate (sub-)plans to achieve them[12]. This
axiom is represented formally as follows:

$$\textbf{RG 8.} \models \begin{bmatrix} (Has\_plan\ x\ p\ \varphi) \wedge \\ (\textsf{GOAL}\ x\ \varphi) \wedge \\ (\textsf{BEL}\ x\ \langle pre(p)\rangle) \wedge \\ (Choose\ x\ p\ \varphi) \end{bmatrix} \Rightarrow (\textsf{INTEND}\ x\ \langle body(p)\rangle).$$

Although this formalism avoids many of C&L's drawbacks, the branching
nature of worlds makes modelling the interaction between beliefs, goals and
intentions very complex. For example, the compatibility axioms require that
a formula that an agent has as a goal or an intention be an O-formula. An
O-formula is one that when converted to its positive normal form, consists
of only optional operators but no inevitable operators (e.g., $E \Diamond E(p \wedge q)$,
$E(p\,\mathcal{U}\,q)$, etc.).

2.4.3 Other Formalisms of Intentions

Many other formalisms have aimed to capture the role of intentions in an
agent's behaviour. Among these a selected number which propose some significant properties relevant to the context of this work, will be briefly reviewed.

---

[12] Note that, the authors assume a deliberation function which chooses an appropriate plan for a given situation to achieve an adopted goal, denoted by
$(Choose\ x\ p\ \varphi)$.

Seel's Formalism

Seel [See89] uses a propositional linear discrete-time temporal logic with modalities for knowledge and want (intention). The semantics is given via possible-world semantics. In general there are a set of problem-specific axioms which *prescribe* the behaviour of an agent (called Agent-Axioms), and a set of axioms which *describe* the environment of the agent (called World-Axioms). A legitimate world is a world which satisfies World-Axioms.

The assumption is that agents have epistemic memory, that is, at any given moment i an agent has information available about what happened in states $0, \ldots, i - 1$. Therefore knowledge of an agent is all the *strict-past* formulae. The knowledge of 'what happened in the past', (i.e., evidence and outcome(s)) together with the behaviour axioms, are used to determine what should be done next (i.e., want). However, only if the outcome of a certain evidence has always been the same in the past, an agent would be able to choose its future 'sensibly', (i.e., want it). If the outcome is not uniform in the world states in the past, or that no evidence is available in the past which resembles the current state, then the agent 'is allowed to make a mistake'. But whatever the agent chooses to perform will not be said to be wanted by the agent. As a result, if an agent performs a wanted action it is guaranteed to succeed with it, which contradicts the conceptual intuition about intentions. It intuitively leads to the *side-effect problem* discussed in the previous subsection, since what an agent wants is closed under what it knows to be true. An additional problem with this formalism is that as the axioms prescribing an agent's behaviour are fixed, it is not possible to accommodate changing wants [Sin95].

Singh's Formalism

Singh [Sin95] developed a branching time logic with possible world semantics. Beliefs of an agent at a given time point are given by an interpretation function which assigns to an agent the state of affairs that the agent considers as possible. The theory puts an special emphasis on modelling actions and time. The notion of goal and the action to achieve the goal is subsumed by the notion of '*strategy*' which characterises an agent's behaviour. In other words, strategies are used as an abstract notion for the actions achieving some condition. Intentions of an agent then correspond to the courses of events (strategies) preferred by the agent, i.e. it's preferred scenarios. The author states however, that intentions of an agent are determined not only on the basis of the strategies he is currently following, but also on the basis of the actions he can perform on different scenarios, his *abilities* and *know-how*. The notion of '*know-how*' plays an important role in characterising success and the role of intention as leading to action. Know-how refers to the knowledge of *how* to act and knowledge of skills, which the author distinguishes from '*know-that*' which refers to the knowledge of facts. Having identified and formally defined these constructs, the author moves on to define intentions in communication which will be discussed in Section 2.7.

The definition of belief and intentions obey many of Bratman's requirements. As stated by the author himself, since the theory is an external one, (i.e., the formalism is developed from an observer's perspective), it leaves the design of agents an open issue as long as the design obeys the requirements of intentions, beliefs and know-how. Therefore, this work like Cohen and Levesque's, stays at the theoretical level and does not provide much insight into the design and implementation of agents.

In an earlier work, Singh had given the semantics of beliefs and intentions based on CTL*, but modelled these attitudes using Asher Kamp Discourse Representation framework [SA92], [Sin91a]. The formalism is very rich and considerable effort has been made to capture important properties of beliefs, intentions and communication (see below, on representational approaches).

Representational Approaches

Goldman and Lang [GL93] base their formalism on Allen's [All84] logic of action and time. Allen's logic is an interval-based first-order system. As with C&L they describe persistent goals, relativised goals, intentions regarding actions and relative intentions. But they avoid some of the problems of C&L's formalism by using a syntactic theory as opposed to a modal theory. The important part of their work is that goals and intentions are linked to actions of agents, and the time it takes to perform an action. As with R&G's formalism, goals are distinguished from desires by requiring them to be consistent.

The authors state that use of syntactic theories allow reasoning to be done at a symbolic level, and further more, avoids the problem of consequential closure of modal theories. But as was discussed in Section 2.3 the problem with syntactic theories is the characterisation of the truth or falsehood of propositions by comparing them with the "true" state of affairs. One problem of these definitions is that the persistence of goals and intentions are strictly related to an action that the agent would perform herself. Therefore actions of other agents cannot be taken into account. Secondly, if an action has been performed but failed to achieve the goal, the agent would drop its intention. The problem actually lies in having to formally list all possible conditions of persistent of goals and intentions. The commitment criteria in practice is much more complicated than the theory will have us believe. For instance, one may drop a goal simply because achievement of another (a new) goal has a higher priority for the agent over its currently held goal. Finally the formalism does not account for choices of an agent in terms of the possible means of achieving that goal, by for example delegating its achievement to another agent or achieving it collaboratively with other agents.

Konolige and Pollack [KP93] use a syntactic representation of beliefs and intentions. Their work places emphasis on abilities and intentions in relation to planning, and in this respect is very rich. But as was discussed above and in Section 2.3 although syntactic approaches avoid the problems associated with logical omniscience (mainly closure under logical consequence), they are semantically not as strong as possible world approaches.

2.5 Rationality, Reasoning and Decision Making

In general there are two rather different approaches towards rationality. In philosophy, as characterised by Dennett, rationality means obeying the rules of logic. In practice, this involves developing a system of logic by describing the premises of the system in a set of basic axioms, and then devising inference rules which determine if a particular proposition follows from the given premises. A rational action then is one which the arguments for its selection logically follow from the current beliefs of the agent. The second field is decision theory which models beliefs about what could happen if a given action is chosen, by associating probabilities with each possible outcome, or sequence of outcomes. Desires are modelled by real numbers which represent the utility of those possible states. According to decision theory, a rational action is one that optimises expected utility, which is calculated from the beliefs and desires using probability theory.

Most of the approaches to rationality either assume a logical rationality, or a decision-theoretic rationality. From a conceptual point of view, while the logical approach enables rational *reasoning*, decision-theoretic approach enables rational *decision making* by optimising the fulfillment of subjective utilities. From a technical point of view, with a logical rationality we have symbolic reasoning, but no way to optimise utilities. On the other hand, decision theoretic rationality provides numeric decision analysis methods but neglects the reasoning aspect.

Decision-theoretic methods are not the only methods for decision making. For instance, there are qualitative methods using preferences model, case-based reasoning methods, or modelling the decision criteria in terms of hard and soft constraints that have to be respectively satisfied and optimised. The important fact to note here is that a resource-bounded agent situated in a dynamic domain, should not only be able to reason about its world but also make decisions in order to gain the optimal benefit from the outcome of its actions.

Rao and Gerogeff for example illustrate how their BDI-logic can be utilised with a decision-theoretic approach for decision making [Foo89], [RG91b]. Their logical framework describes the role of intentions in means-end reasoning, but they argue that it is the process of *deliberation* that can lead to the formation of intentions [RG91b]. Both *decision trees* in decision theory and desire-accessible worlds in their framework, capture the desirable ends or outcomes of the decision problem, the different alternatives or choices available to the agent to achieve those ends, and the chance events controlled by nature. This intuitive mapping is possible because possible worlds are represented as branching-time rather than linear-time structures.

By adopting Fagin and Halpern's formalism on reasoning about knowledge and probability, and extending it to the branching-time model, they model probability distribution on belief-accessible worlds. To achieve pay-off distribution on desire-accessible worlds, they introduce a function that associates numeric values with paths on the desire time trees. In other words, by this, they transform probability and pay-off distributions in decision trees to belief- and desire-accessible worlds.

From a possible worlds perspective, this provides a concrete method for obtaining the probability and pay-off distribution on the worlds, and from the decision-theoretic perspective, the transformation facilitates symbolic manipulation of decision-theoretic entities. Hence given a decision tree and the corresponding transformation, an agent can make use of standard decision theoretic techniques such as *maximin* or *maximising expected value* (see [Foo89] to decide the best plan of action, commit to it and thereby adopt an intention.

This book does not commit to any particular method of decision making, and in fact stresses the fact that the choice of particular method should be dependent on its appropriateness to the application domain in question. Nevertheless, it puts a great emphasis on the importance of deliberation on formation of intentions, and for this, not only the logical framework should be expressive enough to allow choices to be explicitly represented, but also a theory expressing the reasoning and deliberation process should define constructs that represent the type of decisions required in the process. This will be further discussed in the next chapter in section 3.4.2.

2.6 Reciprocity

The notion of reciprocity, refers to an agent reciprocating the stance towards other agents. This is a very important step as far as multi-agent systems are concerned. An agent requires to be able to reason about other agents' beliefs, desires, intentions and abilities, in order to co-exist, compete or cooperate with them. This is intuitively a *micro-perspective*, i.e., an agent's perspective of other agents in its surrounding. In this thesis we will narrow our focus to topics related to cooperation and collective activities. In particular, this section will provide a survey of related theories on shared mental states, namely *mutual beliefs, joint goals* and *joint intentions*. It is important to point out that most of the studies in this topic provide a *macro-perspective*, i.e. an observer's perspective on the mental states and activities of a group of agents. This will be discussed further in the next chapter.

It was first in the field of distributed computing, that the need for a theory of knowledge of multiple processes was recognised. In particular, it was found useful for design and analysis of distributed protocols, to express the states of knowledge that the system goes through during the execution of protocols.

Halpern and Moses [HM85] pay a special attention to states of common knowledge of a group of processors. The semantics of common knowledge[13] is given by first defining an operator for 'everyone knows', whose semantics in turn (for n processors) is given as follows:

$$\langle M, w \rangle \models \mathsf{EK}\varphi \quad \text{iff} \quad \langle M, w \rangle \models \mathsf{K}_i\varphi \text{ for all } i \in \{1, \cdots, n\}$$

For a fact to be a common knowledge, each processor must also know that everyone knows that fact, and know that everyone knows that he knows that fact and so on, to some degree k, (i.e. the recursive nesting of knowledge to some degree k):

$$\langle M, w \rangle \models \mathsf{CK}\varphi \quad \text{iff} \quad \langle M, w \rangle \models \mathsf{EK}^k\varphi \text{ for all } k \in \{1, \cdots, \infty\}$$

In a related literature in multi-agent systems, the notion of *mutual belief* is used instead of common knowledge, [RGS92] [KLR$^+$94] [Woo94], [WJ94b]. The definition of mutual beliefs may be generally given as follows:

$$(\mathsf{MBEL}\ g\ \varphi) \overset{def}{=} \bigwedge_{i \in g} (\mathsf{BEL}\ i\ \varphi \wedge (\mathsf{MBEL}\ g\ \varphi)).$$

Therefore a group of agents mutually believes φ, if each agent in the group believes that φ holds and believes that φ is mutually believed by all.

Halpern and Moses have shown that, common knowledge (or mutual knowledge) cannot be attainable if communication is not guaranteed or if there is uncertainty in message delivery time [HM85]. An example of this situation is the famous *coordinated attack problem*, where two troops want to attack the enemy, but neither would attack unless the other troop would attack too. A further remark is made by Singh [Sin91b] who criticises the recursive definitions of belief. He argues that:

> "Not only is the mutual belief requirement computationally demand-
> ing (so that agents may reason about others to arbitrary nesting of
> beliefs), it also requires a lot of communication among the members
> (for the mutual beliefs to be established). ... In practice, they [mutual
> beliefs] can be established only if certain conventions are stipulated."

Many theories rely on mutual beliefs in order to describe shared mental properties of a group of agents without specifying the required conventions. We will refer to this problem later in the next chapter and assume the above definition for mutual beliefs throughout this section.

2.6.1 Joint Intentions: Background

In Section 2.4 it was shown that the major role of intentions is that they move an agent to act, and control the agent's future conduct (see Section 2.4). Similarly, Searle [Sea90] identifies two components to an action (of for example

---

[13] For semantics of knowledge see Section 2.3.

raising an arm): a *"mental"* component and a *"physical"* component. The mental component both represents and causes the physical component. One important benefit of multi-agent systems is that agents can engage in collaborative activities either because no one agent can accomplish the task alone; or in order to obtain a better overall performance. According to the philosophical studies, collaborative activity of a group of agents is also caused by some mental component that ultimately leads the members to act; and controls their conduct in the collaborative activity. Conte [Con89] uses the term *"group minds"* and *"collective unconscious"* to refer to this mental component. In this view, group mind is not part of any individual member and is external to the individuals.

A number of researchers use the notions of *we-intentions* [TM88], *group intentions* [Sin91b], or *joint intentions* [CL91] [RGS92] in order to refer to the mental component that represents and causes the actions of the group members in the collaborative activity. In essence, they all attempt to describe joint intentions in terms of individual intentions with mutual belief. This view does not however support Conte's theory that there is a group mind independent of individuals.

Searle [Sea90] also objects to this view of collective intention but on a different ground. He argues that collective intention is not reducible to individual intentions of the group members. In his view, collective intention is a primitive which leads to individuals' intention-to-act, that is, intend the *means* of achieving the collective intention. For example consider two agents who wish to cook a spaghetti sauce together *by means of* one agent putting in the ingredients and the other stirring the sauce. In this case the two agents have the collective intention of cooking spaghetti which leads to individual intentions of putting in the ingredients for one agent and stirring the sauce for the other agent. Searle also rejects Conte's argument by stressing that any theory of collective intentionality must be consistent with the fact that: *"since a society consists of only individuals, there cannot be a group mind or group consciousness. All consciousness is in individual minds, in individual brains."*

It appears that in talking about collective activities, we are dealing with two phenomena: (i) an external phenomenon that exists outside individual members' mind, which controls the group's activity before and after collaboration commences, and prescribes the code of conduct within the group, and (ii) an internal phenomenon that exists inside individual members' mind which leads to individual's action as part of achieving the collective goal. In other words, there is a social/organisational/macro phenomenon and an individual/micro phenomenon.

Conte and Chastelfranchi [CC93] focus on the notion of *norms* as the key issue. Norms provide rules of conduct for a group of agents (e.g., how things are normally done in an organisation). They identify two types of norms: (i) those which are aimed at improving the agents' performances (e.g. the traffic norms), and (ii) those which are intended to reduce what they call *"displayed aggression"* (e.g. norm of reciprocation). They denote that norms are a social as well as a mentalistic notion. They see norms as the key element linking individual agents to the collective minds and social structures, in other words they see norms as the missing micro-macro link.

Jennings talks of individual's *responsibility* [Jen92] towards the group members and argues for certain general *conventions* that the team members should obey. A convention is described as

> *"... kind of meta-level plan, that provides abstract guidance for the actions of agents engaged in cooperative action. It describes the circumstance under which an agent should review its progress towards a joint goal, and indicates course of action to follow if, for example, problems are detected, or the goal is achieved."* [WJ94b].

It appears that norms and conventions are the type of external phenomenon that exist with respect to group activities. In other words, norms and conventions are separate phenomena, independent of the states of individual agents' minds (i.e. wishes, beliefs, desires, intentions and so forth). They bind the individuals' actions into a coherent group activity. Joint intentions on the other hand are internal phenomenon. They lead to actions of the individual members of the group. It is the *knowledge* of the existing norms and conventions that are internal to the agents, whether they are explicitly encoded as part of the definition of joint intentions or implicitly in the description of group activity.

In the formalisms presented in the next subsection, some authors treat joint intentions as a separate notion from the conventions and the norms involved in collaborative activities (see for example [RGS92]), and some explicitly integrate norms and conventions as part of the definition of joint intentions (see for instance [Jen93] and [WJ94b]).

2.6.2 Joint Intentions: Formalisms

The common view of joint activity is that of a group of agents having an objective (shared or adopted) that they wish to achieve collaboratively. This definition helps to distinguish a joint goal from a parallel goal. For example agent a and agent b may both have the goal of going for a day-trip, but only if they both wish to go *together*, is the goal a joint one, otherwise they have parallel goals. Having a joint goal however, does not necessarily lead to a joint intention and consequently to a joint activity. There are many questions that need to be addressed with regards to collective activity. Cohen and Levesque [CL91] for instance address the following problems:

- How joint beliefs, goals and intentions of a team lead to those of the individuals so that anything gets done?

- How do joint intentions to perform complex actions lead to appropriate intentions to perform the pieces?
- Assuming that an agent will only intend to do her own actions, what is her attitude towards the others' share?
- Which of the characteristic roles of individual intentions outlined by Bratman (see Section 2.4), also apply to the team?
- What do agents need to know (and when) about the overall activity, about their own part, and about the other agents' shares?
- Should agents communicate when the joint actions is to begin, when one agent's turn is over, when the joint action is finished, when the joint action is no longer needed?
- How does communication facilitate the monitoring of joint intentions?

In modelling *joint intentions*, Bratman identifies the following requirements (c.f. [RGS92]):

1. *Commitment to joint activity*: team members be committed to executing their respective parts of a joint plan of action. But the individual agents not be coerced to adopting the joint intentions. That is, there has to be a 'willingness' from the part of team members. Implicit in this account is agreement of the team members to a common solution, in other words, agreement of the team members to the joint plan and each agent's respective parts, or role in the plan.
2. *Mutual responsiveness to a goal*: team members share a joint goal and the joint intention is a means of achieving the joint goal.
3. *Commitment to mutual support*: the team members be committed to communicate the success or failure of their actions to other team members. In general, obligations and entitlements flow from an agent's readiness to act jointly.

Any theory of joint intentions should state how these requirements may be formulated and in doing so describe how the questions like the ones stated by Cohen and Levesque may be answered. In the following, a brief account of some of the existing theories on joint intentions and cooperative activities will be discussed with a reference to if and how each theory fulfills any of the above requirements.

Tuomela and Miller

Tuomela and Miller [TM88] use the notion of *we-intentions* as the mental attitude pre-requisite to a collective activity. Central to this theory is the strong requirement that group members should share a common objective for the activities that they undertake. In this view, therefore, even if an agent in a group performs a helpful act but is unaware of the overall goal, he is not actually participating in a group activity. Informally, an agent A who is a member of a group "we-intends" to do X if:

1. Agent A intends to do his part of X,
2. A believes that the preconditions of success obtain; especially, he believes that other members of the group will (at least probably will) do their parts of X.
3. A believes that there is a mutual belief among the members of the group to the effect that the preconditions of success mentioned in part 2 obtain.

This account attempts to reduce collective intentions to individual intentions plus mutual beliefs. Searle objects to this definition by stating that a group can satisfy these conditions and still not exhibit a collective behaviour. Searle notes that the notion of a we-intention of collective intentionality, implies the notion of *cooperation*. Although cooperative collective goals may be pursued by individualistic means (i.e. individual intention to act), the mere presence of I-intentions to achieve a goal that happens to be believed to be the same goal as that of other members of a group does not entail the presence of the intention to cooperate to achieve that goal. In agreeing with Searle's non-reductive position with respect to joint intentions, Tuomela attempts in a later article [Tuo94] to demonstrate that their theory of we-intentions is not reductive.

The theory of we-intentions, also lacks an adequate reference to the representation of collective actions, joint plans, and agreement of the team members on the joint plan and the role of each participant in the plan. Although these are recognised they are not explicitly represented in their theory. Hence it seems that the theory of we-intentions only partly fulfills Bratman's first and second requirements with no reference to the third requirement, namely commitment to mutual support.

Grosz and Sidner

Grosz and Sidner [GS90] adapt Pollack's [Pol90] model of beliefs and intentions, and use 'plans' as recipe of actions to achieve certain ends. They focus on modelling collaboration and dialogue, and therefore instead of joint intentions they model *shared plans* which exist between the group. Their definition of shared plans like we-intentions in [TM88] does not seem to capture the important property of joint intentions, in that a group may have a shared plan without ever collaborating.

Levesque and Cohen

Levesque and Cohen's work on team activity [LCN90], [CL91] is primarily concerned with developing a reasonable specifications for joint activity, rather than characterising some natural concept of joint activity. In other words, specifying properties that a design should satisfy, and that would then lead to a desirable behaviour. In their approach, they investigate in what ways a team is in fact similar to an aggregate agent and as a consequence, to what extend their theory of individual intentions (see Section 2.4.1) can be carried over to the joint case. Their model of mental states of individuals is a belief-goal-commitment in which intentions are specified not as a primitive mental feature, but as *"internal commitments to perform an action while in a certain mental state."* Analogously they argue for a notion of joint intention, which is formulated as a *"joint commitment to perform a collective action while in a certain shared mental state"* as the glue that binds team members together. But they note that joint commitment cannot be simply a version of individual commitment where a team is taken to be a single agent. If an agent comes to believe that a goal is not achievable, then she must give up the goal. Similarly when a member of a team finds out that a goal is not achievable, the team as a whole must give up the goal, but the team does not necessarily know enough to do so. They state that before a joint commitment can be discharged, the agents must in fact arrive at the mutual belief that the termination condition holds. To capture this, they define *weak achievement goal* of each team member nominally working on the goal. Informally, an agent x has a weak achievement goal relative to another member y to bring about φ, if either (i) agent x has a normal achievement goal to bring about φ, that is, the agent does not yet believe that φ is true and has φ eventually being true as a goal, or (ii) the agent believes that φ is true or will never be true, but has as a goal that the status of φ be mutually believed by all the team members.

They then define *joint persistent goal* of agents x and y relative to a condition ψ to achieve φ, if they mutually believe that (i) φ is currently false; (ii) they both want φ to eventually be true; and (iii) φ is a mutual (achievement) goal, until the status of φ is mutually known to both agents.

Similar to the definition of individual intentions, joint intention is defined to be a joint commitment to the agents' having done a collective action, with the agents of the primitive events as the team members in question, and with the team acting in a joint state. Hence, a team of agents jointly intends, relative to a condition, to do an action if and only if the members have a joint persistent goal relative to that condition of their having done the action and, moreover, having done it mutually believing throughout that they were doing it.

Although the theory provides some insights as to how the formalism of individual intentions may be extended to joint intentions, it suffers from the same weaknesses as with their formalism of individual intentions. Moreover, the theory does not account for many important requirements of group activity such as team formation, plan generation, joint plan agreement, role assignment and synchronisation that will be discussed later.

Rao, Georgeff and Sonnenberg

The formalisation of joint intentions presented in [RGS92] is based on Rao and Georgeff's earlier work on belief, desire and intention of individual agents which was briefly reviewed in Section 2.4.2. Instead of referring to a group of agents, the authors use a recursive notion of a *social agent*. A social agent is a set of other social, or individual agents, e.g., team, organisation and so on.

They also define mutual beliefs (also joint goals and joint intentions) as individual beliefs (resp. individual goals and intentions) with mutual belief. An important property of their formalism is that the strong realism constraint (see Section 2.4.2) also apply on joint attitudes:

RG 9. $\models (\mathsf{JINTEND}\ \tau\ \varphi)\ \Rightarrow (\mathsf{JGOAL}\ \tau\ \varphi)$
$\Rightarrow (\mathsf{MBEL}\ \tau\ \varphi)$

The authors make use of pre-compiled *social plans* which are syntactic entities that are invoked by a *social agent* in particular situations to satisfy certain ends. These ends are achieved by different agents synchronising their actions as specified by the structure of the social plan. Each plan (individual or social) specifies *how to carry out the plan* (called the *body* of the plan), and *under what conditions such a plan can be usually executed* (called *precondition* of the plan). They state that it is important to know who has the plan and what the plan accomplishes. This is denoted by (*Has_plan x p φ*), where x, p and φ respectively refer to an agent, a plan and a condition which the plan accomplishes.

The process of means-end analysis with respect to cooperative activities, involves choosing a joint goal that needs to be satisfied, selecting a social plan, and finally jointly intending a social plan. This may also involve communication between agents and synchronisation of adoption of joint mental attitudes and joint actions of agents.

The scenario for a social agent is very similar to the single-agent case described in Section 2.4.2 (RG8), by considering joint attitudes rather than the individual ones:

$$\models \left[\begin{array}{ll} (\textit{Has\_plan}\ \tau\ p\ \varphi) & \wedge \\ (\mathsf{JGOAL}\ \tau\ \varphi) & \wedge \\ (\mathsf{MBEL}\ \tau\ \langle pre(p)\rangle) & \end{array} \right] \Rightarrow (\mathsf{JINTEND}\ \tau\ \langle body(p)\rangle)$$

It is important to note that there is no 'choose' function specified for the multiple agent scenario. Hence it is not stated how agreement to a common solution or a joint plan is reached. It appears that the authors assume that for any joint goal there is either only one social plan, or that each individual agent's 'choose' function would choose the same joint plan for the given situation and joint goal.

The authors state that their theory of social plans and joint intentions captures Bratman's first requirement, namely, commitment to a joint activity, but not the '*willingness*' part of it. They suggest that non-coercion may be enforces by restricting the object of a joint intention to be a joint social plan, but they also note that this approach is unsatisfactory, because what constitutes coercion or non-coercion would then depend on the plan library of the agent and would not be a property of his intentions. The second requirement, namely, mutual responsiveness to a goal, has also been captured, but not the third requirement (i.e., commitment to mutual support). The authors argue that commitment to communication or any obligation is a consequence of adopting joint intentions and is not part of the definition of joint intentions.

Kinny et al.

The work on social plans in [RGS92] has been extended in [KLR+94], emphasising on the specific problems involved in plan execution by a team. In this regard they list the following problems:

- how to find a suitably qualified team for a task (*team formation*).
- how to synchronise the adaptation of joint goals and intentions (*mind-set synchronisation*).
- how to assign responsibilities for different parts of a plan to members of a team (*role assignment*).
- how to maintain proper temporal relationship between the execution of parts of a plan for different team members (*role synchronisation*).
- how to select between alternative plans (*plan selection*).
- how to behave in the event of plan failure.

Team formation, plan selection and role assignment are guided by knowledge about the skills and plans of agents and teams. This knowledge is assumed to be known at compile-time. *Plans* of a team are the intersection of plan library of the team members. *Skills* of a team are the set of primitive actions that can be performed by the team. Individual agents may have different skills, and composite teams may have skills not possessed by their members. *Role* of a team member in the plan, is the part of the plan to be undertaken by that team member.

The definition of joint intentions of a team towards a plan is refined in terms of the joint intentions and mutual beliefs of the *role-players* of the joint plan towards respective role-plans. Hence a team τ has a joint intention towards a plan p, if:

1. every role-player has the joint intention towards the plan;
2. every role-player believes that the joint intention is being held by the team; and
3. every role-player believes that all role-players executing their respective role-plans results in the team executing the joint plan.

According to the authors, under this formalism all the three requirements for joint intentions stated by Bratman are met. The holder of a joint intention has beliefs about the parts to be played in the joint activity by the members of the team, has a joint goal that the team is accomplishing, and has a responsibility to communicate the success or failure of its actions at various stages of the joint activity to others in the team. There are however many assumptions in the work, which over-simplifies the processes involved before joint intentions can be formed. These are discussed below:

1. The theory of joint attitudes is heavily based on the structure of pre-compiled social plans, where roles and skills are decoded in the syntax of the plans. Furthermore, skills and plans of agents are a common knowledge, also previously compiled by the designers of the system. As a result, the reasoning behind team formation, role assignment and mind set synchronisation and so forth are too crude and simplistic.

2. Inherent in the structure of social plans is the temporal relationship between actions and subplans which simplifies role synchronisation.

3. Normally there are two reasons for an agent to want to achieve his goal collaboratively: (i) he does not have the required resources (such as skills, plans, other physical resources etc.), or (ii) it would benefit more from achieving his goal collaboratively [HS93]. In this framework, the evaluation of whether an agent can or cannot accomplish a goal on his own is dependent on whether the plan corresponding to the accomplishment of the goal is an individual or a social plan. Therefore, this framework does not permit situation based evaluations for making such decisions. Such a requirement seem to be shifted by assuming a deliberation function which chooses an appropriate plan (assuming that the plan library has both an individual and a social plan for achieving the same goal), but the theory does not address it explicitly.

As a concluding remark, the results of this work with regards to the practical aspects of joint intentions and cooperative activity are very encouraging. However, since the processes involved in reaching agreements heavily rely on certain assumptions that are more related to design and architectural issues, the framework is too restrictive in its applicability as a general theory of reasoning about joint activity.

Wooldridge and Jennings

The formal framework of Wooldridge and Jennings [WJ94b] draws upon and extends the work in [LCN90], [RGS92], and [KLR+94]. The language of formulation resembles Cohen and Levesque's language [14] [CL90], but extends it into a quantified branching time logic[15]. In this survey, because of space limitations, the formalisms will be discussed only informally. A complete formal treatment may be found in [WJ94b].

Commitment and *conventions* are the basis of their formalism of cooperative problem solving. While commitment is a pledge or promise by the participants to a course of action or a state of affairs, conventions provide a set of abstract guidelines as to how the participants should behave in the cooperative activity. They view conventions as a set of rules, each rule consisting of a re-evaluation condition ρ and a goal γ. The idea is that if ever an agent believes ρ to be true, then it must adopt γ as a goal, and keep this

---

[14] As a reminder, C&L's language is a first-order multi-modal linear time logic.

[15] For various forms of temporal logic see [Eme90].

goal until the commitment becomes redundant. Therefore, they first give a general definition of joint commitments, parameterised with a set of convention rules. Joint commitments are used to develop a model of joint persistent goals similar to Levesque et al.'s model [LCN90].

Based on Levesque et al.'s work, they define joint intentions towards a cooperative action in terms of joint goals, but joint intentions towards a cooperative action α means having a joint persistent goal that eventually g will believe α will happen next, and then α happens. Therefore an advantage of this work as compared to Levesque et al. is that commitment is strictly future-directed with no 'looking back', that is, it does not mean having a persistent goal of a particular state in the future at which when looking back, the agent had believed that he would do α and after that he did α.

A very important contribution of this work is the model of cooperative problem solving, consisting of the stages:

Recognition: in which an agent identifies the potential for cooperation.
Team formation: in which the agent solicits assistance.
Plan formation: in which the newly formed collective negotiate to construct a joint plan of action.
Execution: in which members of the collective play out the roles they have negotiated.

Considerable effort has been put into formalising these phases, making it theoretically superior to other attempts in formalising cooperative problem solving. But unfortunately, the space does not permit a thorough analysis of this work.

Conceptually, the process of team formation to engage in a cooperative activity shares many insights with the theory of commitments given in the next chapter. Technically, the related formalisation is based on Cohen and Levesque's, while the formalisms that will be developed in the next chapter is based on Rao and Georgeff's model of intentional attitudes. The comparison of the two approaches on the theoretical level have been already discussed in the previous section. One of the problems with Cohen and Levesque's formalism and consequently this formalism is that the theory of joint intentions and cooperative activity are technically so complicated that one cannot immediately see in what way they may be made operational. All the formalisms discussed in the previous section and this section, are based on very complex logics. Because of their complexity, we are far from being able to develop a programming language that could 'execute' such logics and consequently the formalisms based on them. Therefore as far as practicality of the theories are concerned, one can at least hope that any theory of intentional systems identifies the important data structures and clearly defines the relationship between these structures such that they can be used as the ground for the design of cognitive components of agents. For this purpose as well as enabling agents themselves to reason about their own and other agents' beliefs, plans, desires and so forth, it would help if a theory explicitly and clearly describes these attitudes from '*within*", that is from the perspective of different agent's involved and not from '*without*', that is, from the outset observing the system as a whole. As will be argued in the next chapter (and demonstrated in chapter 5), in comparison with Cohen and Levesque's formalism, Rao and Georgeff's formalisms have more practical advantages. The design constructs and control in their abstract BDI-architecture directly reflect the formal constructs and the relationship between them.

2.7 Communication

While reasoning about cooperation relies on modelling other agents as intentional systems, due to the temporal nature of many intentional attitudes as well as the fact that these attitudes are local to the individual agents, the need for communication is at times inevitable. Therefore, after reciprocity Dennett associates the next level of sophistication to the ability for a "meaningful" communication, which ultimately relies on the preceding steps.

Research in communication in multi-agent systems has in many parts benefited from the insights in Speech Act Theory. By taking advantage of this fact, the survey will start from the inputs of Speech Act Theory into communication among agents.

2.7.1 Speech Act Theory

Speech Act Theory is primarily concerned with natural language utterances. Austin [Aus62], one of the pioneers in this field, noticed that the sentences uttered by human during communication do not always simply assert a fact, but actually perform some action and that utterances accomplish actions by having certain forces. There are three types of actions associated with an utterance:

1. *Locution*: the physical act of uttering the sentence;
2. *Illocution*: the action of conveying the speaker's intent to the hearer; and
3. *Perlocution*: any actions caused as a result of uttering the sentence. This includes (if not limited to) the actions taken by the hearer upon the occurrence of the utterance.

For example, "shut the door" is the actual locution, with the illocutionary force that the hearer shuts the door, and what ever the hearer does as a result is the perlocution. While often a speaker utters a sentence performing an illocution with the aim of achieving a perlocutionary effect, these effects are beyond the control of the speaker.

It appears that in the multi-agent literature, a speech act is mainly associated with its illocution, which is characterised as having two parts: an *illocutionary force* and a *proposition* [Sea69]. The illocutionary force distinguishes for example a *command* from a *promise*, and the proposition describes the state of the world that is, respectively, commanded or promised [Sin95]. Cohen and Levesque [CL88] however argue that the explicit recognition of the illocutionary force by the hearer is unnecessary. Instead, many properties of illocutionary acts can be derived from the speaker's and hearer's mental states, especially from their beliefs, intentions and the common knowledge of the communicating parties about certain conventions. Therefore they aim to employ insights from linguistics theory on human communication to artificial systems, by characterising the conditions under which illocutionary force of an utterance may be *inferred*. For instance the sentence "can you pass the salt" may be inferred as being an indirect request to pass the salt under the conditions that both the speaker and the hearer are aware of this linguistic/social convention. This may be referred to as *indirect speech act* [Sin95]. Unless communicating with a human, reasoning about ambiguities of messages exchanged is unnecessary in artificial systems as long as the semantics of messages are unique to both the senders and receivers of messages. As a result, while locutionary acts may be designed directly and explicitly into the syntax of messages, their illocutionary force must be determined by giving speech acts precise formal semantics.

A more common impact of speech acts is seen in *message types*, initially motivated by Searle's [Sea69] classification of illocutionary forces into *assertives, directives, commissives, permissives, prohibitives* and *declaratives*. Table 2.2 (taken from [Sin95]) provides examples of speech acts with different illocutionary forces.

Table 2.2. Classification of Speech Acts

Force	Example
Assertive	The door is shut
Directive	Shut the door
Commissive	I will shut the door
Permissive	You may shut the door
Prohibitive	I name this door the Golden Gate

Searle's classification suggested that speech acts can be grouped together into classes in such a way that the speech acts in the same class share the same condition of satisfaction. But his classification was criticised basically because its basis of classification is semantically coarse [Lev81], attempting to put together speech acts of varying strengths, and differing pragmatic effects [Sin95]. Ballmer and Brennenstuhl [BB81] for instance attempted to classify all German speech act verbs into Searle's speech act classes. They faced enormous difficulties in this process, as with addition of more verbs, they had to re-analyse all previously classified verbs.

It appears that the problem lies on the basis upon which the conditions of satisfaction of each group may be characterised. There are a variety of pragmatic factors that could take part in this classification such as roles and social statures, norms and conventions of the system and the language, which are in any case difficult to be taken as isolated and general factors to base the classification upon. For example, one could distinguish between a *command* and a *request* in that a command is usually issued to a sub-ordinate, while a request can be issued to almost anyone, although both may be classified under directives. According to Singh [Sin95], *"the constraint on when requests and commands are issued and satisfied may be stated that capture their non-semantic aspects properly"*.

Instead of such a rigid classification, Ballmer and Brennenstuhl [BB81] suggested to group the verbs that are similar in meaning, into *semantic categories*, and group the semantic categories into *models* according to semantic similarity. For example a model of an 'enquiry', consists of a 'question' and an 'answer'. The models also include an ordering of the categories according to their *temporal relationship* and *degree of effectiveness*. For example an 'answer' always comes after a 'question', and 'threatening' is stronger than 'warning'. The categories and the models including the temporal ordering between them not only provide a more pragmatic categorisation of speech acts, but also suggest that semantics of communication must be studied in the form of dialogues rather than single messages in isolation.

In multi-agent systems, dialogues and the related interactions are designed into protocols that will be discussed next.

2.7.2 Interaction Protocols

A number of researchers have proposed protocols and frameworks to support cooperation in specific multi-agent scenarios. To mention a few, the well known Contract Net Protocol [Smi80], [DS83], the hierarchical protocol [DM90], PERSUADER [Syc88] and so forth. The protocols proposed have been mostly concerned with a unique method of cooperation and the possible negotiation steps within that method. For instance, the Contract Net Protocol is designed for task-allocation, the hierarchical protocol of Durfee et al. is aimed at coordination, and the rest are specific unique protocols for negotiation.

To describe cooperation in multi-agent systems, deGreef et al. [dGCM92] have devised a general specification language that is transformable into an already implemented language. The purpose of this language is to abstract away from details which are not relevant to the interacting agents, so that designers can easily define the interaction knowledge. If this language is as claimed general enough for specification of all types of cooperation methods, its merits are doubtless. Nevertheless, of benefit would be some means by which cooperation methods can be conveniently developed from their components and consequently analysed and experimented at a more abstract level.

Winograd and Flores [WF86] use a network of speech acts consisting of straightforward conversations for action. Their aim is at structuring dialogues and analysing conversations. Some authors have used graphical representations to express their individual cooperation methods, example of which are negotiation protocols in [KvM91] and SANP (Speech Act Negotiation Protocol) in [CW92]. Campbell and D'Inverno [CD90] proposed a general graphical representation for defining cooperation protocols. The graphical notations used by all these authors, are basically state transition diagrams, but the meaning of the nodes and the arcs differ from one author to another according to what aspect of cooperation has been of interest. For instance in Campbell and D'Inverno's proposed representation, protocols not only represent the communication between two agents, but also the reasoning states. But this could be only possible if we assume an agreed standard on the classification and semantics of message types. Furthermore, since reasoning and decisions concerning cooperation is highly application-dependent, the internal reasoning mechanisms of agents must be on a separate layer and independent of the level at which dialogues are represented.

In view of this book, in design of protocols as general interaction means, we should be able to fulfill the following requirements:

1. A representation that is intuitive in terms of sketching various states of dialogue, and independent of application domains and their requirements.
2. Protocols must be at a level of abstraction separate from the internal components of individual agents and their reasoning mechanisms. But their representation must explicitly specify the interface to the internal components of the agents.
3. Ideally, it must be possible to design and develop protocols obeying modular design conventions, enabling rapid prototyping for analysis and experimentation.

Motivated by these requirements, chapter 5 (Section 5.6) describes the concept *cooperation protocols* [BHS93] as a general means of designing and analysing dialogues in pairwise interactions. But this is only at the level of dialogue design and representation. There is certainly more to communication than simple syntactic utterances in dialogues. Singh [Sin95] for instance has developed a theory to capture an objective semantics of the messages exchanged, by specifying the satisfaction conditions of speech acts in Searle's classification. For instance, his theory specifies that "*a directive is satisfied just if (1) its proposition becomes true at a moment in the future of its being said, and (2) all along the scenario from now to then the hearer has the know-how, as well as the intention to achieve it.*".

He states that his theory is an objective criteria with which to evaluate the correctness of the different scenarios that are the possible runs of executions of a multi-agent system. But he also includes that we require *prescriptive* specifications that tell agents what to do given their beliefs and intentions, so that only correct scenarios may emerge. This nicely captures one of the objectives of this book and will be discussed in chapter 4.

Therefore, to achieve meaningful dialogues, we require to specify under what conditions individual agents may choose to perform a particular speech act. In this book, these conditions are specified in terms of beliefs, goals and intentions of individual agents and their belief about the intentional states of their communicating partners. Messages or rather communicative actions will not however be considered in isolation, but in the context within which a dialogue may take place, and according to the rules and conventions governing the interactions in that context. This means that reasoning about communication does not only involve reasoning about when and what speech act to perform, but also what is involved after a message is received, (i.e., the perlocutionary effects of the speech act).

2.8 Discussion

This chapter provided a literature review of the related philosophical and theoretical background to agents as intentional systems, with various levels of sophistication, namely, one that possess certain mental attitudes and reasons based on these attitudes, one that can model and reason about other agents by taking an intentional stance towards them, and one that is capable of meaningful communication.

The purpose of this chapter was to motivate that designing such systems should ground on a full-fledged formal theory, and not an ad-hoc principle. There are many diverse approaches to formalising intentional attitudes, seemingly with diverse objectives. Basically these objectives may be divided into micro and macro perspectives, that is, theories that try to analyse and capture how a group, an organisation, or a society behaves as a whole, and theories that try to specify the internal component and reasoning mechanisms of individual agents that enable them to behave in certain desired ways, as part of that whole.

The objective of this book falls mainly into the latter category, attempting to realise what attitudes constitute the internal components of an agent and what the relationship between these components are. A survey of literature reveals that in general beliefs, desires, goals, plans, intentions and preferences are taken as representatives of classes of intentional attitudes whose roles with respect to computational agents are more or less understood. Bratman's philosophy identified the relationship between beliefs and intentions and between intentions and other motivational attitudes such as desires and preferences. These distinctions have provided the basis for many of the formalisms that have attempted to capture characteristic properties of intentional attitudes.

This chapter described and made comparisons between some of the existing theories not only based upon how well a theory captures these properties, but most importantly, given the objective of this book, how closely the corresponding theory allows the intentional components and their relationship to be mapped to their operational components. Based on this, it appears that Rao and Georgeff's BDI-framework comes closest to this objective.

The remainder of this chapter provided an overview of the studies related to communication in multi-agent systems. In this regard, many inputs to the research in communication has come from Speech Act Theory. With communication one is not only concerned with the syntax of messages but also with their corresponding actions and purpose (i.e., semantics). Furthermore, communication should not only be limited to isolated messages and their interpretation but should be studied in the framework of dialogues and the context of interactions. But underneath dialogues lies the reasoning and decision making mechanisms that operate on the intentional attitudes of individual agents and their belief about the intentional attitudes of other agents. With this in mind, chapter 4 will attempt to provide a specification of this mechanism based on the theory of commitments that will be developed in the next chapter.

In conclusion, just like Dennett had characterised, the basic levels of sophistication in characterising an intentional system are the interplay of intentionality, rationality and stance. Any theoretical or practical approaches to modelling intentional systems with increasing levels of sophistication will have to deal with all the underlying levels and integrate them into the higher levels. And this is what we intend to accomplish in this book.

3. A Formal Theory of Commitments

3.1 Overview

This chapter aims at developing a formal theory of individual and joint commitments. The theory takes an internal perspective to model how individual agents may reason about their actions. The formalism developed is based on Rao and Georgeff's BDI formalism to model individual agent's intentional attitudes [RG91c]. The theory of joint commitments is developed by extending this formalism. The related reasoning constructs in the theory are formulated within the framework of a specific convention introduced to control agent interactions in the process of engaging in a possible cooperation.

This chapter is mainly divided into three parts. Section 3.2 motivates the approach, Section 3.3 introduces the logical framework, and Section 3.4 develops the theory of joint commitments. Since the theory is intended to be pragmatic, the theory of joint commitments will be described as an integral part of the means-end reasoning processes of agents. Finally, Section 3.5 concludes this chapter.

3.2 Background

The philosophical and theoretical studies of agents as intentional systems have revealed many insights into the interplay of intentional attitudes and their role in "rational" behaviour. In particular, they have revealed that mental attitudes provide an appropriate level of abstraction for modelling and experimenting with the cognitive capabilities of agents. Chapter 2 provided a survey of several logical frameworks devised to capture characteristic properties of these attitudes. The perspective taken by the theories that have exploited these issues fall into two categories: *external perspective* where the formalisms are described from an observer's perspective on individual agents and a group of agents; and *internal perspective*, where the formalisms are described from the perspective of individual agents on their own internal states, their environment and the other agents. External theories are said to be more *descriptive*, in that the studies undertaken by such theories tend to describe and analyse when an agent or a group of agents could be said to *have had* certain mental states, based on their observed behaviour. Most of these theories do not provide a basis for the rational *formation* and execution of intentions [GI88]. The *internal* theories, on the other hand, are said to be more *prescriptive*, since the formation of certain mental states and how they lead to the individual or groups' activity is mostly prescribed (somewhat subjectively), by the designer of the system. On the theoretical level, there are debates on the validity of the *descriptive* verses *prescriptive* argument. Perhaps a fairer argument as noted in [WJ94b], is that while external theories concentrate more on developing theories *about* agents, internal models concentrate more on developing models which might be used *by* agents. An internal theory would typically identify the key data structures of an agent and the relationships between these structures.

In relation to cooperation and collective activities, as was demonstrated in Section 2.6.1, we are concerned with both the *micro* and *macro* aspects of artificial agency [Sho94], where the micro aspects are concerned with the mental state, rationality, and communication acts of a single agent; and macro aspects refer to the society of agents with social laws and conventions among them. While the micro aspects help to design individual reasoning agents in a society of agents, the macro aspect, helps to design appropriate interaction laws that should govern the society. Therefore, it seems reasonable to model the micro aspects with an internal perspective, and analyse and experiment with different models concerning the macro aspects with an external perspective.

The main focus of this work is to specify the reasoning processes that guide communicative activities of agents towards a potential cooperation. Like any other activity, this reasoning is part of the *means-end reasoning* [BIP88] of an agent, i.e., choosing the appropriate means of achieving some desired ends. The idea is that the *need* for cooperation should arise from individuals' mind (their beliefs, goals and intentions) and thereafter individual attitudes towards a possible cooperation be communicated. Therefore the work concentrates mostly on the micro aspects of agency. Nevertheless, the reasoning involved in interactions should be constrained by the laws and conventions of the society, and influenced by roles of the individuals within the community. Therefore certain laws and conventions must be established to guide and control the group activity before and after collaboration commences. Clearly, although such macro properties are external to the individual agents, they still need to be internalised to the individual agents.

This chapter introduces the formal framework within which the means-end reasoning and subsequently the reasoning behind interactions will be described. This framework allows formulae to be expressed with an internal perspective. The logical system adopted is based on the belief, desire, intention (BDI) model of Rao and Georgeff (see Section 2.4.2) [RG91c], and inherits almost all the semantic conditions and related axioms of their model. Using this logical apparatus, we define certain important reasoning constructs and outline the relationships between them. These constructs will be used in the next chapter to characterise the reasoning states that lead to communication acts of agents to negotiate about a possible future cooperation.

3.3 The Logical Framework

The language of formulation $\mathcal{L}$, is a first-order, multi-modal, branching-time logic. It is largely similar to the language of formulation employed by Rao and Georgeff in [RG91c], which is a first-order variant of CTL* (Computational Tree Logic) [Eme90].

Formulae of the language are evaluated in a world. Informally, a world is considered as a time-tree, with a single past and a branching future. This allows two types of formulae to be expressed in the language: *state formulae*, which are evaluated on a given time point in a given world, and *path formulae*, which are evaluated at a given path (sequence of time points) in a given world.

In addition to the usual operators of first-order logic: ($\neg$ (not), $\vee$ (or), $=$ (equality), and $\exists$ (existential quantifier)); the language provides the temporal operators $\bigcirc$ (next), $\Diamond$ (eventually), $\mathcal{U}$ (until); and the path operator E (some path) of branching time logic, modal operators for *belief, goal* and *intention*, and a number of other operators that will be informally described below.

The formulae (BEL x φ), (GOAL x φ) and (INTEND x φ) mean: agent x has a belief of φ, has a goal of φ, and intends φ respectively. The language imposes a KD45 logic (modal system weak-S5) on belief, and KD logic (modal system D) on goals and intentions [Che80].

Actions can only be carried out by agents, and each agent is capable of performing a number of actions. The formula (Agent α x) means that x is the agent of action α. There are a number of operators that apply on actions: (Succeeds α) and (Fails α) are path formulae, which refer to the future success and failure of execution of action α respectively; (Succeeded α) and (Failed α) are state formulae which refer to the past success or failure of execution of action α. These operators also apply on plans.

Each agent is assumed to have a *library* of plans. Each plan is a branching structure, referred to as a *plan expression*. A plan expression can be simply an *action term*; a *test action* represented by φ? (where φ is any state formula); or formed from other plan expressions using the ';' and '|' operators, inspired from dynamic logic [Har79]. The plan expression $\pi_1; \pi_2$ means that plan expression π_2 must be executed after the plan expression π_1, and $\pi_1 | \pi_2$ means either π_1 or π_2 must be executed. The operator (Has_Plan x p φ) is used to denote that agent x has a plan p in his plan library that if executed successfully would achieve φ.

The syntax and semantics of the language will be provided in the subsections that follow[1]. The first subsection gives the symbols and syntax of

---

[1] The presentation of syntax and the semantics is inspired by [Woo92].

the language. For ease of reference, the semantics of the language are given
in three parts: the preliminaries of the language including the structure of a
model within which formulae are evaluated is given in Section 3.3.2; plans and
the semantics of action formulae which apply to actions and plans are given
in Section 3.3.3; the modelling of beliefs, goals, and intentions, is described
in Section 3.3.4.

3.3.1 Syntax of the Language

Symbols of $\mathcal{L}$

1. *propositional connectives* : ¬ (not) and ∨ (or);
   existential quantifier ∃;
   operator symbols : Succeeds, Fails, Succeeded, Failed, Has_Plan, Agent, =;
   modal operators : BEL, GOAL, INTEND;
   path operator : E (optionally);
   temporal operators : ○ (next), ◊ (eventually), and $\mathcal{U}$ (until);
   action operators : '|' (disjoint), and ';' (sequence);
   plan operator : '?' (testing);
   punctuation symbols : ')', '(', ']', '[', '.' and ','.
2. a countable set *Const* of *constant symbols*, the union of the mutually
   disjoint sets $Const_{Ag}$ (agent constants), $Const_{Ac}$ (action constants),
   $Const_P$ (plan constants), and $Const_{Obj}$ (other constants);
3. a countable set *Var* of *variable symbols*, the union of the mutually disjoint
   sets Var_{Ag}, Var_{Ac}, Var_P, Var_{Obj};
4. a countable set *Pred* of *predicate symbols*. Each symbol $q \in Pred$ is
   associated with a natural number called its *arity*, given by $arity(q)$. The
   0-ary predicate symbols are known as *proposition symbols*.

Syntax of $\mathcal{L}$

The notation used to describe various components of this language loosely
adheres to VDM [Jon90].

A *term* is either a constant or a variable; the set of all terms is denoted
by *Term*. The *sort* of a term is either Ag, Ac, P or Obj; if s is a sort then
$Term_s = Const_s \cup Var_s$.

The syntax of the well-formed formulae ($\langle fmla \rangle$) of the language is given
in Figure 3.1.

3.3.2 Semantics of the Language

Preliminaries

First, some informal description of the formal framework is represented. The
world is modelled as a *time-tree*. A time-tree is constructed from an infinite

$$
\begin{array}{rcl}
\langle term \rangle & ::= & \text{any element of } Term \\
\langle ag\_term \rangle & ::= & \text{any element of } Term_{Ag} \\
\langle ac\_term \rangle & ::= & \text{any element of } Term_{Ac} \\
\langle plan\_term \rangle & ::= & \text{any element of } Term_{P} \\
\langle pred\_sym \rangle & ::= & \text{any element of } Pred \\
\langle var \rangle & ::= & \text{any element of } Var \\
\langle plan\_expr \rangle & ::= & \langle ac\_term \rangle \\
& | & \langle state\_fmla \rangle? \\
& | & \langle plan\_expr \rangle \text{ '|' } \langle plan\_expr \rangle \\
& | & \langle plan\_expr \rangle \text{ ; } \langle plan\_expr \rangle \\
\langle ac\_fmla \rangle & ::= & (\textsf{Succeeded } \langle plan\_expr \rangle) \\
& | & (\textsf{Succeeds } \langle plan\_expr \rangle) \\
& | & (\textsf{Fails } \langle plan\_expr \rangle) \\
& | & (\textsf{Failed } \langle plan\_expr \rangle) \\
& | & (\textsf{Has\_Plan } \langle plan\_term \rangle \langle state\_fmla \rangle) \\
\langle state\_fmla \rangle & ::= & \langle pred\_sym \rangle(\langle term \rangle, \cdots, \langle term \rangle) \\
& | & \langle ac\_fmla \rangle \\
& | & (\textsf{Agent } \langle ag\_term \rangle \langle action\_term \rangle \\
& | & (\textsf{BEL } \langle ag\_term \rangle \langle state\_fmla \rangle) \\
& | & (\textsf{GOAL } \langle ag\_term \rangle \langle state\_fmla \rangle) \\
& | & (\textsf{INTEND } \langle ag\_term \rangle \langle state\_fmla \rangle) \\
& | & \neg \langle state\_fmla \rangle \\
& | & \langle state\_fmla \rangle \vee \langle state\_fmla \rangle \\
& | & (\langle term \rangle = \langle term \rangle) \\
& | & \exists \langle var \rangle . \langle state\_fmla \rangle \\
& | & \textsf{E} \langle path\_fmla \rangle \\
\langle path\_fmla \rangle & ::= & \langle state\_fmla \rangle \\
& | & \neg \langle path\_fmla \rangle \\
& | & \langle path\_fmla \rangle \vee \langle path\_fmla \rangle \\
& | & \exists \langle var \rangle . \langle path\_fmla \rangle \\
& | & \bigcirc \langle path\_fmla \rangle \\
& | & \Diamond \langle path\_fmla \rangle \\
& | & \langle state\_fmla \rangle \; \mathcal{U} \; \langle state\_fmla \rangle \\
\langle fmla \rangle & ::= & \langle state\_fmla \rangle
\end{array}
$$

Fig. 3.1. Syntax of the Language

set T of *time points* and a binary relation $\prec$ on T, which represents all possible courses of world history: $t \prec t'$ iff the time point t could be transformed into time point t' by occurrence of a primitive action that is possible in t. The relation $\prec$ will therefore *branch* infinitely into the future from every time point. It is however, assumed that each world has a single past (see [RG91c]), and as a result, $\prec$ is backwards-linear. Since a time point is transformed to another time point by the occurrence of actions, each arc in $\prec$ is associated with an action given by a total mapping $Act: \prec \longmapsto U_{Ac}$.

The world is populated by a non-empty set U_{Ag} of agents and other objects (e.g., books, cups, etc.) given by the set U_{Obj}. Agents can perform certain actions. The set of all the actions is represented by U_{Ac}. Actions can only be performed by agents, and the function Agt returns the agent of an action. The set U_P contains all possible plan expressions over U_{Ac}. Each agent owns a subset of the plans U_P, and function Π returns the set of plans owned by an agent. This subset is called the *plan library* of the agent.

Agents can communicate with one another by *sending* and *receiving messages*. Sending and receiving messages are also primitive actions in U_{Ac}. The set of messages is denoted by MSG, where each message is a tuple composed of a *message-type*, a sender, a receiver and the fact (called *content*) that is communicated. The set MT is a finite set of message types, each represented by a string of characters. We assume the existence of another language $\mathcal{L}'$ for formulating the *content* of messages.

Agents have beliefs, goals and intentions, given by *belief, desire* and *intention-accessibility* relations respectively, which will be extensively discussed in Section 3.3.4.

Next we will discuss the technical apparatus for dealing with the denotation of terms.

Definition 1. *The domain of quantification U is $U_{Ag} \cup U_{Ac} \cup U_P \cup U_{Obj}$.*

Definition 2. *A variable assignment V, is the mapping $V : \mathrm{Var} \longmapsto U$. A constant interpretation C, is a sort preserving bijection $C : \mathrm{Const} \longmapsto U$.*

Definition 3. *A term can be either a constant or a variable. We use the following denotation for interpretation of a term:*

$$[\![\tau]\!]_{C,V} \stackrel{def}{=} \begin{cases} C(\tau) & \text{if } \tau \in Const \\ V(\tau) & \text{otherwise.} \end{cases}$$

Definition 4. *A model M is a structure:*

$$M = \langle W, T, U, MT, MSG, \prec, Act, Agt, \Pi, \mathcal{B}, \mathcal{D}, \mathcal{I}, C, \Phi \rangle$$

where:

- W is a set of worlds (see the next definition);
- T is a non-empty set of time points (otherwise known as states or situations);
- U is the domain of quantification (see above);
- MT is a set of message types:
    {*inform, query, demand, command, request, offer, propose, accept, reject, report*};
- $MSG = MT \times U_{Ag} \times U_{Ag} \times \textit{wff}(\mathcal{L}')$
    is a set of messages, where $\textit{wff}(\mathcal{L}')$ is any well-formed formula of the communication language $\mathcal{L}'$;
- $\prec \subseteq T \times T$
    is a binary relation between adjacent time points where $\langle T, \prec \rangle$ is an infinite time-tree[2]. The temporal precedence relation $\leq$ on T is then defined to be $\prec *$. This relation is transitive and backwards-linear.
- $Act : \prec \longmapsto U_{Ac}$
    associates a primitive action with each arc in $\prec$;
- $Agt : U_{Ac} \longmapsto U_{Ag}$
    gives the agent of each primitive action;
- $\Pi : U_{Ag} \longmapsto powerset(U_P)$
    gives the plan library of each agent;
- $\mathcal{B} \subseteq U_{Ag} \times W \times T \times W$
    is a transitive, Euclidean, serial relation which maps an agent's current situation to a set of worlds called belief-accessible worlds[3].
- $\mathcal{D} \subseteq U_{Ag} \times W \times T \times W$
    is a desire-accessibility relation which mapping an agent's current situation to a set of worlds called desire-accessible worlds.
- $\mathcal{I} \subseteq U_{Ag} \times W \times T \times W$
    is a serial relation, mapping an agent's current situation to a set of worlds called intention-accessible worlds.
- $C : Const \longmapsto powerset(U)$
    is an interpretation for constants; and finally
- $\Phi : Pred \times W \times T \longmapsto \bigcup_{(n \in I\!N)} powerset(U^n)$,
    gives the extension of each predicate symbol in each situation, such that:
    $\forall q \in Pred . \forall n \in I\!N . \forall t \in T . \forall w \in W . (arity(q) = n) \Rightarrow \Phi(q, w, t) \subseteq U^n$.

---

[2] We assume the formal definition of trees in Graph Theory

[3] Note that in effect $\mathcal{B}$ is a relation mapping $(U_{Ag} \times W \times T)$ to W, and it is this relation that is transitive, Euclidean, and serial. Similarly for $\mathcal{D}$ and $\mathcal{I}$.

Definition 5. *A world $w \in W$ (called a time-tree) is a tuple:*

$$w = \langle T_w, \prec_w, Act_w, \mathcal{E}_w \rangle$$

where:

- $T_w \subseteq T$, is a set of time points in world w.
- $\prec_w$, is the same as $\prec$, restricted to time points in T_w.
- Act_w, is the same as Act, restricted to the relations between time points in T_w.
- $\mathcal{E}_w : \prec_w \longmapsto \{'s', 'f'\}$,
  is a arc labelling function that for each agent maps adjacent time points to one of $'s'$ (for success) or $'f'$ (for failure).

A *fullpath* in a world w is an infinite sequence of time points $(t_0, t_1, ...)$, such that $\forall i \in \mathbb{N}, t_i \in T$. $t_i \prec_w t_{i+1}$. The notation $(w_{t_0}, w_{t_1}, \cdots)$ is used to make the world of a particular fullpath explicit. Alternatively we use $\rho_{t_0}^w$ as abbreviation. A *finite* path is represented by ρ_{t_0,t_i}^w to denote a path from time point t_0 to time point t_i in world w. Since there is assumed to be only one past, if the current time point in world w is t, there exists one and only one time point t' such that $t' \prec_w t$.

Semantics of First-Order Formulae

The semantics of first-order *state formulae* is given in a model M, with a variable assignment V and the world w at the current time point t_0:

$$
\begin{array}{llll}
\langle M, V, w_{t_0} \rangle & \models & q(\tau_1, \cdots, \tau_n) & \text{iff} \quad \langle [\![\tau_1]\!], \cdots, [\![\tau_n]\!] \rangle \in \Phi(q, w, t_0) \\
\langle M, V, w_{t_0} \rangle & \models & (\text{Agent } \alpha\ x) & \text{iff} \quad [\![x]\!] = Agt([\![\alpha]\!]) \\
\langle M, V, w_{t_0} \rangle & \models & \neg\varphi & \text{iff} \quad \langle M, V, w_{t_0} \rangle \not\models \varphi \\
\langle M, V, w_{t_0} \rangle & \models & \varphi \vee \psi & \text{iff} \quad \langle M, V, w_{t_0} \rangle \models \varphi \ or \ \langle M, V, w_{t_0} \rangle \models \psi \\
\langle M, V, w_{t_0} \rangle & \models & (\tau_1 = \tau_2) & \text{iff} \quad [\![\tau_1]\!] = [\![\tau_2]\!] \\
\langle M, V, w_{t_0} \rangle & \models & \mathsf{E}\varphi & \text{iff} \quad \exists \rho_{t_0}^w \ s.\,t. \ \langle M, V, \rho_{t_0}^w \rangle \models \varphi \\
\langle M, V, w_{t_0} \rangle & \models & \exists i \,.\, \varphi & \text{iff} \quad \langle M, V\dagger\{i \longmapsto d\}, w_{t_0} \rangle \models \varphi \\
& & & \quad \text{for at least } d \in U \ s.t. \\
& & & \quad \text{i and } d \text{ are of the same sort.}
\end{array}
$$

(Note that $V\dagger\{i \longmapsto d\}$ is the interpretation identical to V except that i is assigned value d.)

The semantics of the first-order *path formulae* is given in a model M, with respect to a variable assignment V and world w on a path starting at the current time point t_0:

$$\langle M, V, \rho_{t_0}^w \rangle \models \varphi \qquad \textit{iff} \quad \langle M, V, w_{t_0} \rangle \models \varphi$$

$$\langle M, V, \rho_{t_0}^w \rangle \models \neg\varphi \qquad \textit{iff} \quad \langle M, V, \rho_{t_0}^w \rangle \not\models \varphi$$

$$\langle M, V, \rho_{t_0}^w \rangle \models \varphi \vee \psi \qquad \textit{iff} \quad \langle M, V, \rho_{t_0}^w \rangle \models \varphi \ \textit{or} \ \langle M, V, \rho_{t_0}^w \rangle \models \psi$$

$$\langle M, V, \rho_{t_0}^w \rangle \models \exists i \,.\, \varphi \qquad \textit{iff} \quad \langle M, V\dagger\{i \longmapsto d\}, \rho_{t_0}^w \rangle \models \varphi$$
$$\text{for at least } d \in U \text{ s.t.}$$
$$\text{ı and } d \text{ are of the same sort}$$

$$\langle M, V, \rho_{t_0}^w \rangle \models \bigcirc \varphi \qquad \textit{iff} \quad \langle M, V, \rho_{t_1}^w \rangle \models \varphi$$

$$\langle M, V, \rho_{t_0}^w \rangle \models \Diamond \varphi \qquad \textit{iff} \quad \exists t_k \,.\, t_0 \leq t_k \ s.\,t. \ \langle M, V, \rho_{t_k}^w \rangle \models \varphi$$

$$\langle M, V, \rho_{t_0}^w \rangle \models \psi \,\mathcal{U}\, \varphi \qquad \textit{iff} \quad \exists t_k \,.\, t_0 \leq t_k \ s.\,t. \ \langle M, V, \rho_{t_k}^w \rangle \models \varphi; \ and$$
$$\forall t_j \,.\, t_0 \leq t_j < t_k, \ \langle M, V, \rho_{t_j}^w \rangle \models \psi$$

The logical operators 'and' ($\wedge$), 'implies' ($\Rightarrow$) and the universal quantifier 'forall' ($\forall$), are defined in the usual way. The temporal operator 'always' ($\square$) and the path operator 'inevitable' (**A**) are defined in terms of their respective counterparts.

$$\square\varphi \stackrel{def}{=} \neg\Diamond\neg\varphi$$

$$\mathbf{A}\varphi \stackrel{def}{=} \neg\mathbf{E}\neg\varphi$$

The axiomatisation of the path operator **A** is based on KT5 (modal system S5) [Sti88]. Axioms of temporal operators and the related inference rules are provided in Appendix A.

Finally, we use the following abbreviation, a variant of the *before* operator in temporal logic, meaning: if sometime in the future φ holds, before that ψ should hold.

$$\psi \,\mathcal{B}\, \varphi \stackrel{def}{=} \Diamond\varphi \Rightarrow \Diamond(\psi \wedge \Diamond\varphi).$$

We do not use the usual definition of the *before* operator (i.e., $\bigcirc\varphi \Rightarrow (\psi \,\mathcal{U}\, \varphi)$) because We require this operator to denote subgoals in a plan of achieving a higher level goal. As will be discussed in the next two subsections, a plan is intended in order to achieve a particular goal. Since a plan body is a tree structure, each sub-tree in the body of a plan achieves a particular subgoal, but a subgoal may not need to (or in some circumstances must not) *remain* true until the higher level goal is achieved. So if an agent has φ as a goal, and ψ is the goal that will be satisfied by successful execution of a particular subtree in the plan of achieving φ, with the usual definition of the *before* operator (i.e., $\Diamond\varphi \Rightarrow (\psi \,\mathcal{U}\, \varphi)$), ψ must remain true at least until φ becomes true. But in practice this is undesirable. For instance, if φ expresses the state of being in the airport, and ψ is the status of waiting in front of the house for a Taxi, then we can't expect to remain waiting in front of the house and in the next state being in the airport.

3.3.3 Actions and Plans

Here we give the syntactic definition of plans and primitive communicative plans, and then give the semantics of *action formulae* for success and failure of primitive actions and plans.

Informally, a plan *denotes* a finite tree structure, called a *plan expression*. A plan expression is either a single action ($\alpha \in U_{Ac}$); a test action ($\varphi?$), where φ is a state formula[4]; or formed from other plan expressions using the operators ';' (for sequencing) and '|' (for non-deterministic actions). For instance, $\pi_1; \pi_2$ means that the plan expression π_2 should be executed after the plan expression π_1 is executed; and $\pi_1|\pi_2$ means either π_1 or π_2 should be executed. (Note that p is a denotation of a plan in the domain U_P, whose structure is a plan expression, whereas π is used to refer to any plan expression that may constitute a plan in U_P).

Inevitably, an unfolded structure of a plan resembles a finite time-tree, where arcs are associated with actions, branches correspond to non-deterministic actions (i.e. choices) and a finite path in the tree corresponds to the occurrence of a sequence of actions.

Before giving the semantics of action formulae for success and failure of actions and plans, the primitive communication plans will be defined. These plans are called primitive, since they are the building blocks of more complex plans. Like actions and plan expressions, complex communication plans (called *protocols*) can be constructed from these primitive plans using the ';' and '|' operators. (See the next chapter for more details).

Definition 6. *A primitive communication plan is a special type of plan where the structure of the plan in this case is restricted to one of the following:*

- send(msg)
- send(msg_1) ; wait ; receive(msg_2)

Here 'send' and 'receive' are primitive communicative actions, 'wait' is a null action[5], and msg, msg_1, $msg_2 \in MSG$. For example, msg is of the form (msg-$type$, sender, receiver, φ), where φ is a well-formed formula of the communication langiage $\mathcal{L}'$, a subset of $\mathcal{L}$. For convenience we use the functions msg-$type(msg)$, $sender(msg)$, $receiver(msg)$ and $content(msg)$, which given a message msg, return the message type, sender, receiver and the content of msg, respectively.

Although communication in principle concerns at least two agents, one may expect a communicative plan to express both the sending of a message and its receipt by another agent. Here we assume that a message sent by an agent is received by the agent who is the recipient of the message, and that the sending agent believes that the recipient has received the message (see the next chapter for more details).

Having given the syntax of plans (object-level and communicative), we now give the semantics of action formulae that operate on these plans.

---

[4] The formula φ is restricted to exclude E and A operators.

[5] The null action *wait* is "executed" until a message is received. This can be expressed in dynamic logic using *while* construct, but to simplify the formulations we assume its intuitive meaning.

Semantics of Action Formulae

Informally, action formulae for success, failure and execution of a plan are defined as follows:

. (Succeeds p) and (Succeeded p) denote future and past successful execution of plan p.
. (Fails p) and (Failed p) denote future and past failure execution of p.
. (Happens p) and (Happened p) denote that p happens next, and p has just happened.
. (Does x p) and (Did x p) denote that agent x executes p next, and x just executed plan p.

Since a plan p denotes a plan expression in U_P, and a plan expression consists of actions and other (sub-plan) expressions, we first give the semantics of the action formulae on actions, then on plan expressions and finally on plans. These formulae are interpreted in model M and variable assignment V, that are omitted hereafter for readability.

1. Actions (i.e., $\alpha \in U_{Ac}$):
   The formal semantics of success and failure of actions is given as follows:
   $$\rho^w_{t_0,t_n} \models (\text{Succeeds } \alpha) \quad iff \quad t_0 \prec_w t_n, and$$
   $$[\![\alpha]\!] = Act_w(t_0,t_n) \text{ and } \mathcal{E}_w(t_0,t_n) = 's'.$$
   $$w_{t_n} \models (\text{Succeeded } \alpha) \quad iff \quad \exists\, t_0 \in T_w, s.t.\ t_0 \prec_w t_n, \text{ and}$$
   $$[\![\alpha]\!] = Act_w(t_0,t_n) \text{ and } \mathcal{E}_w(t_0,t_n) = 's'.$$
   The semantics of past and future failure of actions is defined similarly, except that function $\mathcal{E}_w(t_0,t_n)$ should return 'f' to denote the failure of the action.
   To denote the success or failure of an action executed by an agent x, we use the following abbreviation:
   $$(\text{Succeeds } x\ \alpha) \stackrel{def}{=} (\text{Agent } \alpha\ x) \wedge (\text{Succeeds } \alpha).$$

2. Plan expressions:
   The formal semantics of future success of plan expressions is given as follows:
   $$\rho^w_{t_0,t_n} \models (\text{Succeeds } x\ \varphi?) \quad iff \quad w_{t_0} \models \varphi.$$
   $$\rho^w_{t_0,t_n} \models (\text{Succeeds } x\ \pi_1|\pi_2) \quad iff \quad \rho^w_{t_0,t_n} \models (\text{Succeeds } x\ \pi_1)\ or$$
   $$\rho^w_{t_0,t_n} \models (\text{Succeeds } x\ \pi_2).$$
   $$\rho^w_{t_0,t_n} \models (\text{Succeeds } x\ \pi_1;\pi_2) \quad iff \quad \exists t_i . t_i \in T_w\ s.t.\ t_0 \leq t_i < t_n, \text{ and}$$
   $$\rho^w_{t_0,t_i} \models (\text{Succeeds } x\ \pi_1)\ and$$
   $$\rho^w_{t_i,t_n} \models (\text{Succeeds } x\ \pi_2).$$
   The semantics of failure and past success of plan expressions are defined similarly.

3. Plans ($p \in U_p$):
   The semantics of future success of plans is given as follows:
   $$\rho^w_{t_0} \models (\text{Succeeds } x\ p) \quad iff \quad \exists t_n \in T_w, s.t.\ t_0 < t_n, \text{ and}$$
   $$\rho^w_{t_0,t_n} \models (\text{Succeeds } x\ [\![p]\!]) \quad (where\ p \in Term_P).$$

Other action formulae are defined syntactically as presented below:

$$\begin{aligned}
(\text{Happens } p) &\stackrel{def}{=} (\text{Succeeds } p) & \vee & \quad (\text{Fails } p). \\
(\text{Happened } p) &\stackrel{def}{=} (\text{Succeeded } p) & \vee & \quad (\text{Failed } p). \\
(\text{Does } x \, p) &\stackrel{def}{=} (\text{Succeeds } x \, p) & \vee & \quad (\text{Fails } x \, p). \\
(\text{Did } x \, p) &\stackrel{def}{=} (\text{Succeeded } x \, p) & \vee & \quad (\text{Failed } x \, p).
\end{aligned}$$

Finally, we give the semantics of the action formula: (Has_Plan x p φ) which denotes, agent x has plan p in his plan library to achieve the state of affairs φ.

$$\begin{aligned}
w_{t_0} &\models (\text{Has\_Plan } x \, p \, \varphi) \quad \textit{iff} \quad [\![p]\!] \in \varPi([\![x]\!]) \textit{ and} \\
& \qquad\qquad w_{t_0} \models \mathsf{A} \,\square \,((\text{Succeeded } x \, p) \Rightarrow \varphi).
\end{aligned}$$

Some useful abbreviations that will be used later are as follows: (Achieves x φ) denotes that next agent x will carry out some plan to achieve φ; and (Achieved x φ) denotes that agent x has just carried out a plan and has successfully achieved φ. Note that the former does not guarantee that after p is executed, φ will be successfully achieved. Formally:

$$\begin{aligned}
(\text{Achieves } x \, \varphi) &\stackrel{def}{=} \exists p \,.\, (\text{Has\_Plan } x \, p \, \varphi) \wedge (\text{Does } x \, p). \\
(\text{Achieved } x \, \varphi) &\stackrel{def}{=} \exists p \,.\, (\text{Has\_Plan } x \, p \, \varphi) \wedge (\text{Succeeded } x \, p).
\end{aligned}$$

3.3.4 Belief, Desire and Intention

The semantics of beliefs, desires (and goals) and intentions of an agent in terms of possible worlds with branching time interpretation that will be presented here is largely adopted from Rao and Georgeff's work in [RG91c] and which will be used through out this chapter. A brief account of this work and the comparison with other approaches has already been presented in Section 2.4.2, the semantics of these attitudes and the related axioms and constraints will be elaborated further in this section.

Beliefs are modelled by associating a set of belief-accessible worlds to each situation. Similarly, desires, and goals of an agent are modelled by associating a set of desire-accessible worlds to each situation. Intentions are also modelled in this way using an intention accessibility relation. Let us first give the formal semantics of beliefs, goals, and intentions. Note that goals are distinguished from desires and this distinction will be explained later. For now, it suffices to say that an agent has a set of desire-accessible worlds, and the semantics of goals are given based on these desire-accessible worlds. The set of belief-accessible worlds of an agent x from world w at time t, is denoted by $\mathcal{B}_t^w(x)$, where $\mathcal{B}_t^w(x) = \{w' \mid \mathcal{B}(x, w, t, w')\}$. Similarly we use $\mathcal{D}_t^w(x)$, and $\mathcal{I}_t^w(x)$ to denote the set of desire-, and intention-accessible worlds of agent x in world w at time t, respectively.

$$\langle M, V, w_t \rangle \models (\text{BEL } x \; \varphi) \qquad \textit{iff} \quad \forall w' \in \mathcal{B}_t^w(x), \; \langle M, V, w_t' \rangle \models \varphi.$$
$$\langle M, V, w_t \rangle \models (\text{GOAL } x \; \varphi) \qquad \textit{iff} \quad \forall w' \in \mathcal{D}_t^w(x), \; \langle M, V, w_t' \rangle \models \varphi.$$
$$\langle M, V, w_t \rangle \models (\text{INTEND } x \; \varphi) \quad \textit{iff} \quad \forall w' \in \mathcal{I}_t^w(x), \; \langle M, V, w_t' \rangle \models \varphi.$$

Starting with beliefs, let us examine what all these worlds and above semantics tell us. The belief worlds of an agent are the worlds that the agent believes to be possible. Referring to Figure 3.2, $b1$ and $b2$ are two such worlds believed to be possible in $w0$ at time t_1. The reason for having multiple belief-accessible worlds is to allow different worlds (possibilities) to be modelled in cases where the agent lacks enough information (or is uncertain) about the state of the world. At time t_1 for example, the agent is not certain whether ϕ_2 holds.

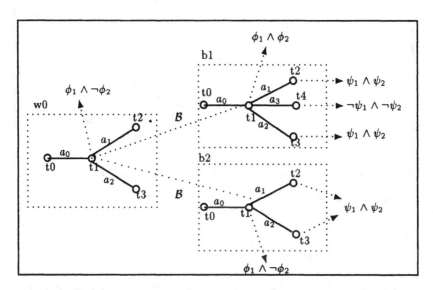

Fig. 3.2. Belief accessible worlds

Each of these worlds are time trees, where branches represent the *choices* or options available to the agent in selecting actions. As the belief relation is time-dependent, the mapping of $\mathcal{B}$ at some other time point, say t_2, may be different from the one at t_1. Thus the agent can change his beliefs about the options available to him. From the semantics of beliefs, a formula is said to be believed at time t by an agent in a world w, if and only if it holds in all his belief-accessible worlds at that time point. Hence at time t_1 in world $w0$, (BEL $x \; \phi_1$) and $\neg$(BEL $x \; \phi_2$) hold. Also at time t_1, (BEL x E $\Diamond \; \psi_1$) and $\neg$(BEL x E $\Diamond \; \psi_2$) hold in world $w0$.

The belief-accessibility relation is serial, Euclidean and transitive, (as demonstrated below) and therefore its axiomatisation is weak-S5 (i.e., KD45) [Che80].

Serial

$$\forall w . (w \in W), \; \exists w' \; s.t. \; w' \in \mathcal{B}_t^w(x).$$

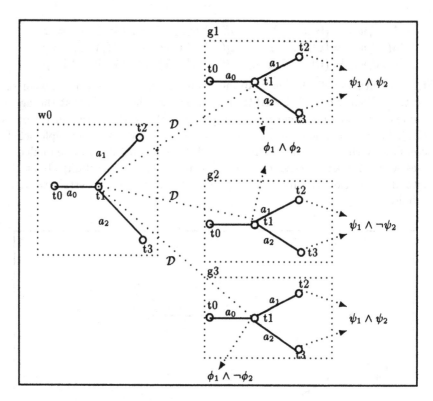

Fig. 3.3. Desire accessible worlds

Euclidean
$$\forall w, w', w'' \in W \quad if \quad w' \in \mathcal{B}_t^w(x) \quad and \quad w'' \in \mathcal{B}_t^w(x) \quad then \quad w'' \in \mathcal{B}_t^{w'}(x).$$
Transitive
$$\forall w, w', w'' \in W \quad if \quad w' \in \mathcal{B}_t^w(x) \quad and \quad w'' \in \mathcal{B}_t^{w'}(x) \quad then \quad w'' \in \mathcal{B}_t^w(x).$$

Desire-accessible worlds model an agent's desires and goals in a given time. For example, referring to Figure 3.3, it is possible for an agent to have both the desire of optionally achieving ψ_1 and ψ_2 by doing α_1 or α_2. Goals, however, are distinguished from desires in two ways: (i) while desires may be inconsistent with one another, goals have to be consistent, in other words goals are *chosen* desires of an agent that are consistent; (ii) the agent should believe that the goal is achievable. The semantics of goals, given above ensures requirement (i), that is, an agent is said to have a goal to achieve a formula at time t in world w, if and only if the formula is true in all his desire-accessible worlds at that time point. Therefore in our example, at time t_1 in world $w0$, the agent can only have the goal to optionally[6] achieve ψ_1, i.e., (GOAL x E $\Diamond$ ψ_1). The requirement (ii) is enforced by the *belief-goal*

---

[6] In this example we could even make a stronger claim that the agent has the goal of *inevitably* achieving ψ_1.

compatibility axiom (Axiom 1) which states that if an agent adopts an O-formula[7] as a goal, the agent believes that formula. That is, if an agent has a goal that optionally he is going to do an action then he also believes that he will optionally do it. (Note that φ in all the axioms that will follow is an O-formula).

Axiom 1. Belief-Goal Compatibility

$$(\text{GOAL } x \ \varphi) \Rightarrow (\text{BEL } x \ \varphi).$$

To model this semantically, we require that for every belief-accessible world from w at time t, there be a desire-accessible world w' such that w' is a subworld of w. Using the operator $\subseteq_{sw}$ for *subworld*[8], this requirement is captured by Constraint 1.

Constraint 1. $\forall w' \in \mathcal{B}_t^w(x) . \exists w'' \in \mathcal{D}_t^w(x) \ s. \ t. \ w'' \subseteq_{sw} w'$.

The reverse, however, need not hold. For instance, in our example, $g1 \subseteq_{sw} b1$ and $g3 \subseteq_{sw} b2$, but $g3$ is subworld of no belief world. As with multiple belief worlds, multiple desire worlds result from uncertainty of an agent about the state of the world. In our example, for instance $g1$ and $g2$ result from the agent's uncertainty about the result of actions α_1 and α_2 in bringing about ψ_2. One desirable property of this model is that, although an agent may believe that ψ_2 is always true whenever ψ_1 is true, i.e. (BEL $x \ \psi_1 \Rightarrow \psi_2$), it need not have ψ_2 as a goal. This is called the *strong realism constraint* and was discussed in Section 2.4.2 in chapter 2.

While goals of an agent represent his *chosen* desired states, and possible paths that lead to those states, intentions of an agent represent his *chosen* future paths to follow, in other words *commitment* to certain *chosen* means (or plans) to achieve those goals. Referring to Figure 3.3, the agent can achieve the goal state ψ_1 by either doing α_1, or α_2. In other words, it can be said that the agent has both the goal of doing α_1 and the goal of doing α_2, but it can only commit to doing of one of these actions. As demonstrated in Figure 3.4, at time point t_0 the agent is committed to doing action α_1 at time t_1. Since like $\mathcal{B}$, the accessibility relations $\mathcal{D}$ and $\mathcal{I}$ are time-dependent, the mapping of $\mathcal{I}$ at some other time point, say t_1, may be different from the one at time t_0, allowing the agent to change his mind and commit to some other action (for example α_2) at time t_1, (see later 'goals, intentions and their parameters' for more discussion).

Both desire- and intention-accessibility relations are serial and therefore their axiomatisation is KD. This means that goals and intentions have to be closed under implication and have to be consistent, (see Section 2.3).

---

[7] R&G [RG91c] define the well-formed formulae that contain no positive occurrences of 'inevitable' (A) outside the scope of the modal operators BEL, GOAL, or INTEND *O-formulae*; and those that contain no positive occurrences of 'optional' (E), *I-formulae* (see Section 2.4.2).

[8] The operators for subworlds are defined in an unpublished article by Rao and Gerogeff.

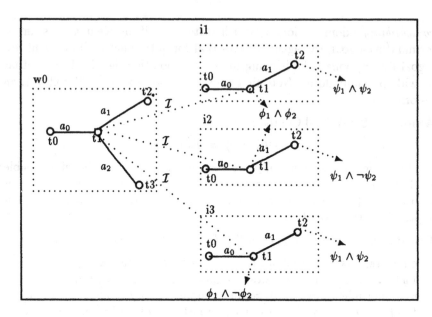

Fig. 3.4. Intention accessible worlds

Similar to the belief-goal compatibility axiom (Axiom 1), there is a *goal-intention compatibility* axiom (presented below), to ensure that if an agent intends a formula, he must also have it as a goal, and therefore from the belief-goal compatibility axiom, he must also believe that it is achievable.

Axiom 2. Goal-Intention Compatibility

$$(\text{INTEND } x \; \varphi) \Rightarrow (\text{GOAL } x \; \varphi).$$

This is modelled by the following constraint, which states that for all the desire-accessible worlds w' from world w, there is an intention accessible-world w'' from world w, such that w'' is a sub-world of w'.

Constraint 2. $\forall w' \in \mathcal{D}^w_t(x) \, . \, \exists w'' \in \mathcal{I}^w_t(x) \; s. \, t. \; w'' \subseteq_{sw} w'.$

Thus, one moves from a belief-accessible world to a desire-accessible world by *desiring* future paths and states of affairs, and from a desire-accessible world to an intention-accessible world by *committing* to a certain desired future path.

To demonstrate the strength of these modal operators with respect to one another, R&G introduce the axioms 3, 4, and 5 presented below, which because of space restrictions will not be discussed in greater detail in this work:

Axiom 3. Beliefs about Goals

$$(\text{GOAL } x \; \varphi) \Rightarrow (\text{BEL } x \; (\text{GOAL } x \; \varphi)).$$

Constraint 3. $\forall w' \in \mathcal{B}_t^w(x)$ and $\forall w'' \in \mathcal{D}_t^w(x)$ we have $w'' \in \mathcal{B}_t^{w'}(x)$.

Axiom 4. Beliefs about Intentions

$$(\text{INTEND } x\ \varphi) \Rightarrow (\text{BEL } x\ (\text{INTEND } x\ \varphi)).$$

Constraint 4. $\forall w' \in \mathcal{B}_t^w(x)$ and $\forall w'' \in \mathcal{I}_t^w(x)$ we have $w'' \in \mathcal{B}_t^{w'}(x)$.

Axiom 5. Goals about Intentions

$$(\text{INTEND } x\ \varphi) \Rightarrow (\text{GOAL } x\ (\text{INTEND } x\ \varphi)).$$

Constraint 5. $\forall w' \in \mathcal{D}_t^w(x)$ and $\forall w'' \in \mathcal{I}_t^w(x)$ we have $w'' \in \mathcal{D}_t^{w'}(x)$.

Following Bratman's analysis of intentions (see Section 2.3), they introduce the following axiom to ensure that intentions do not persist forever:

Axiom 6. No Infinite Defferal

$$(\text{INTEND } x\ \varphi) \Rightarrow \text{A} \lozenge \neg(\text{INTEND } x\ \varphi).$$

This brings us to the subject of persistence and revision criteria for goals and intentions. In this respect, we take Singh's [Sin95] view in that outlining these conditions in a general theory is not adequate, since these conditions are highly dependent on the actual application domain. Furthermore, unlike [CL90] and [WJ94b], we take the view that the revision criteria should not be stated as part of the semantics of intentions. In this view, stating such criteria in a set of axioms like R&G's axioms of change (i.e., blind, single- and open-minded commitment axioms[9]) seems more appropriate. However, the particular commitment strategies to be adopted must be introduced as axioms in the theory of the application in question [RG91c].

Goals, Intentions and their Parameters

Syntactically, both goals and intentions have two parameters: an agent and a well-formed formula of the language. This well-formed formula may be simply a state of affairs, like for example "block b on block a", or an action formula like (**Does** $x\ \alpha$), where α is for example "lift block b". Various formulae may be expressed as a goal or an intention. Referring to Figure 3.5, assuming that g_1 is the only desire-accessible world to agent x at time t_0, x may have the following goals:

1. (GOAL x Eφ) states that x has φ as a goal.
2. (GOAL x E(Achieves $x\ \varphi$)) states that x has it as a goal to execute an action (or a plan) to achieve φ *himself*. In other words, x has it as a goal to execute an action that would achieve φ. In parallel he could still have the goal that some other agent achieves φ, in this example for instance, (GOAL x E(Achieves $y\ \varphi$)) also holds.

---

[9] These are the Axioms RG4, RG5 and RG6, presented in Section 2.4.2.

3. (GOAL x E(Does x α_1)) states that x has it as a goal to execute action α_1. In this case the action is stated explicitly, but not the state of affairs that the successful execution of the action will bring about. In parallel, agent x could also have the goal of achieving φ by other actions, in this example for instance, (GOAL x E(Does x α_2)) also holds.

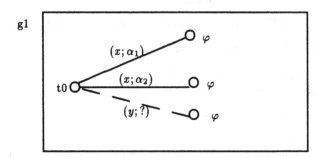

Fig. 3.5. An Example

The main distinguishing factor between intentions and goals is that intentions represent selected goal states and selected future paths that potentially lead to those states. An important characteristic of intentions is that they should move an agent to act. In the formalism, it is assumed that an agent can do only one (primitive) action at a time. Hence, if he has a choice of actions, he needs to deliberate and choose one of them, in order to act *intentionally*. In the example above for instance, if at the current state (t_0), both (GOAL x E(Does x α_1)) and (GOAL x E(Does x α_2)) hold, agent x has to choose and *commit to the doing* of one of these actions. This means that we require that at the time of execution, either x intends (Does x α_1) or (Does x α_2), To ensure this we introduce the following axiom[10]:

Axiom 7. Intentions leading to Actions

$$(\text{INTEND } x \text{ A} \Diamond (\text{Does } x \text{ } \alpha)) \Rightarrow \text{A} \Diamond (\text{Does } x \text{ } \alpha)$$

The formula (INTEND x A(Does x α)) means, in all intention-accessible worlds of x at time t_0, the first arc of all the paths emanating from t_0 are associated with action α, that is: $\forall w' . w' \in I_{t_0}^w$, and $\forall t_1 \in T_w$, s.t. $t_0 \prec_{w'} t_1$, $[\![\alpha]\!] = Act_{w'}(t_0, t_1)$, and $[\![x]\!] = Agt([\![\alpha]\!])$.

If we assume that only a unique action transforms a time point into another time point, then in fact in all the intention-accessible worlds w' at time t_0, all the paths emanating from t_0 share the same first arc (i.e., (t_0, t_1)).

---

[10] This is analogous to R&G's corresponding axiom, in that it ensures there is only one action intended at a time of execution. It is only technically different, because of the slightly different semantics used for future success and failure of actions.

An agent may commit to the doing of many plans in order to achieve a certain state of affairs. It is worth remembering that an unfolded structure of plans resembles a bounded branching time structure.

Let us now examine what it means for an agent to commit to the execution of a plan, for example, (INTEND x A(Does x p)). This formula means that at the current time point, agent x has the intention of only executing plan p. Since a plan can be a branching structure, at the current time point his intention accessible worlds are images of the plan structure, each world differing from others on the outcome of the actions within the plan. However, due to the *intentions leading to actions* axiom, at the time of execution of an action in the plan, if the current plan expression is for example $\alpha_1|\alpha_2$, the agent should choose only one of these actions, in order to act intentionally.

There are two important theorems that relate goals and intentions to achieve a state of affairs individually, to the agent's plans. The first theorem (Theorem 1) states that whenever an agent has a goal to achieve φ individually, he must believe that he has a plan in his plan library that if executed successfully would achieve φ, and that he must have it as a goal to execute that plan.

Theorem 1.

$$\models (\text{GOAL } x \text{ E(Achieves } x \text{ } \varphi)) \Rightarrow \exists p \cdot \left[\begin{array}{l} (\text{BEL } x \text{ (Has\_Plan } x \text{ } p \text{ } \varphi)) \wedge \\ (\text{GOAL } x \text{ E(Does } x \text{ } p)) \end{array} \right].$$

Proof: By expanding the left-hand side of the above implication formula, using the semantics of goals and Achieves given in the previous subsection, we have:

$$w_{t_0} \models (\text{GOAL } x \text{ E(Achieves } x \text{ } \varphi)) \text{ iff}$$
$$\forall w' \in \mathcal{D}^w_{t_0}(x), \ \exists p \cdot (\quad w'_{t_0} \models (\text{Has\_Plan } x \text{ } p \text{ } \varphi), \text{ and}$$
$$\exists \rho^{w'}_{t_0} \text{ s.t. } \rho^{w'}_{t_0} \models (\text{Does } x \text{ } p) \ ).$$

which is in effect, the following logical equivalence:

$$(\text{GOAL } x \text{ E(Achieves } x \text{ } \varphi)) \Leftrightarrow \exists p \cdot \left[\begin{array}{l} (\text{GOAL } x \text{ (Has\_Plan } x \text{ } p \text{ } \varphi)) \wedge \\ (\text{GOAL } x \text{ E(Does } x \text{ } p)) \end{array} \right].$$

Using the belief-goal compatibility axiom (Axiom 1), we can derive the above theorem. $\square$

A similar theorem can be derived for intentions:

Theorem 2.

$$\models (\text{INTEND } x \text{ E(Achieves } x \text{ } \varphi)) \Rightarrow \exists p \cdot \left[\begin{array}{l} (\text{BEL } x \text{ (Has\_Plan } x \text{ } p \text{ } \varphi)) \wedge \\ (\text{INTEND } x \text{ E(Does } x \text{ } p)) \end{array} \right].$$

3.3.5 The Logical System

Let us call the logic described here Γ. This logic inherits all the axioms and inference rules of first-order branching temporal logic[11] outlined in appendix A. But Γ also includes modalities for beliefs, goals and intentions. The axiomatisation of beliefs is KD45 and for goals and intentions is KD. For these attitudes we also have the inference rule of necessitation. In other words, the agent believes, desires (has goals), and intends all valid formulae and therefore all the tautologies. This constitutes Rao and Georgeff's basic BDI-system [RG91b].

In general combining axiomatisations of various logics into a single system of logic is not trivial. We come across the completeness problem. Needless to say, with such logics proving completeness, if at all possible, is an extremely complex task. All we can aim for is to show that our system is sound.

The axioms introduced in the previous subsection, (namely Axiom 1 to Axiom 7), are built on top of the *basic* BDI-system. These axioms basically describe the '*static*' interaction between these modalities, that is, they determine the relationship among different mental attitudes at the same time point.

Hence the system of logic that will be used hereafter, consists of axioms of first-order temporal logic, in addition to the axioms of beliefs, goals and intentions and their static relationships. This system is used to develop a theory for reasoning about means of achieving a goal individually or cooperatively. This theory will mainly specify the dynamic interaction between these modalities restricted to the context of reasoning about a specific type of cooperation.

3.4 Means-End Reasoning

The process of means-end reasoning involves reasoning about how to achieve a goal state in a given situation. The means to an end may be decided to be carried out individually (as in single-agent systems), or cooperatively. The types of cooperative activity considered in this book are restricted to *task delegation* and *task adoption*. In its simplest form, task delegation refers to delegation of achievement of a goal to another agent, and task adoption refers to adoption of achievement of another agent's goal. Task delegation and adoption are important and integral parts of the process which leads to cooperative problem solving of a group of agents.

The means-end reasoning process can be expressed by the expression "*chance + choice + commitment*" [RG93]. While chances refer to the possible future states of the environment, choices correspond to the decisions an

---

[11] The full axiomatisation of first-order CTL* has not been developed. The axioms and inference rules associated to this logic are therefore only a known subset.

agent makes based on what it believes to be possible and desires to bring about. For individual task achievement, an agent's commitment (or individual intention) expresses *when* an agent pursues a *chosen* course of action and *under what conditions* he should give up his commitment to those choices. In terms of cooperative activity, as was discussed in Section 2.6.2, we are also concerned with commitments that are often referred to as *joint intentions* to achieve a joint goal. In our internal theory such a joint goal is the goal that is delegated or adopted, according to the perspective taken. Such a commitment requires that the two agents agree on the terms of cooperation and mutually believe that they both wish to cooperate. Hence before making a commitment, or in fact in order to arrive at a mutual belief about each other's attitude towards a potential cooperation, the participants may need to communicate, and possibly to negotiate. This communication results from the different reasoning states that an agent finds itself in during the process of means-end reasoning.

The theory that will be developed in the remainder of this chapter, aims at characterising these reasoning states within the boundaries of a specific convention that will be described in the next section. Based on this convention, three important reasoning constructs are identified, namely, *potential for cooperation*, agent to agent *pre-commitments* and *commitments*. This convention and a discussion on commitments in general will be given in the next subsection. Each of the above reasoning constructs are formally defined in Section 3.4.2, and the relationships between them is captured in a number of axioms in Section 3.4.1. Then in a number of theorems, it is shown how much of the common intuitions of joint commitments are captured in our theory.

3.4.1 Commitment

When considering the concept of commitment, be it an individual commitment to achieve a state of affairs or execute a plan (i.e., an individual intention), a commitment of one agent to another agent in the context of task delegation and task adoption, or more generally joint intentions of a group of agents to engage in a cooperative activity, we are confronted with the following questions:

1. What conditions need to be maintained while being committed? (*maintenance conditions*)
2. Under what conditions is a commitment formed? (*formation conditions*)
3. Under what conditions should an agent re-consider his commitment? (*revision conditions*)
4. What should the agent do after he gives up a commitment? (e.g., *responsibilities*).

The existing approaches to commitment that are based on Cohen and Levesque's model of intentions, pack the answer to most of these questions into the semantics of intentions. As argued by Singh, this makes it hard to disentangle these different conditions from the semantics in order to state explicitly when an agent intends something *simpliciter* [Sin92], how his intentions are formed, when he should give up an intention, and so on. This was extensively discussed in the previous chapter. Another approach has been to specify the revision conditions not as part of semantics of intentions (*per se*), but in a set of axioms. Rao and Georgeff [RG91a] for instance, have introduced different axioms for different commitment strategies (see Section 2.4.2). These strategies have been experimented with in different environments and the effectiveness of the strategies is empirically compared according to the dynamics of the environment. The authors state that for a single situated agent the number of possible strategies is limited. With respect to commitments in the context of joint activities however, the revision conditions as well as what an agent should do once he gives up a commitment is very much dependent on the individuals' roles and responsibilities characterised by the organisation of the system, its norms and conventions and in general the macro aspects of agency discussed in Section 2.6.1. The approach in [WJ94b] has aimed to incorporate these conventions, but again in the semantics of intentions.

The work presented here specifies some of the general conditions that lead to commitment revision. It however, does not specify what an agent should do once he gives up the commitment. Commitments are given separate semantics and since the revision conditions and the subsequent behaviour of the agents (e.g., their responsibility) are considered mostly as being application specific, they may be introduced further as commitment axioms in the theory of the application in question. In this work we primarily aim at a specification that explicitly characterises the conditions under which a commitment is formed. In our view this is the first important aspect in the design of the reasoning processes of an agent. Unfortunately this is either absent or implicit in the previous theoretical approaches.

Another problem is a technical one. Joint intentions of a group of agents are commonly defined in terms of the mutual beliefs that they all wish to engage in an agreed form of cooperative activity. In practice however, such a state is crucially unachievable if communication is not guaranteed [HM85], but more importantly (as stated by Singh [Sin91b]) these states can be established only if certain conventions are stipulated. Therefore, in our work we take a more pragmatic approach by adopting the following convention:

The Convention: once a *potential for cooperation* is detected, the negotiation process commences. After a series of negotiation steps, eventually one of the negotiating parties (say agent x) finalises his terms of cooperation by making a *pre-commitment*, and communicates this to the other agent (say agent y). This finalisation marks the last steps of negotiation, that is, agent y now must either make a *commitment* or else opt out. We require that if y agrees on the final terms then he makes a *commitment* to x on the agreed terms.

Furthermore, whatever decision y makes at this stage must be communicated to x. If y makes a commitment, after he communicates his commitment to x, x's pre-commitment becomes a full commitment. If y does not agree with the final terms, then both agents will come to believe that a potential for cooperation does not exist on the negotiated terms.

Our theory models this process in terms of the transition between the reasoning states involving *potential for cooperation*, *pre-commitment* and *commitment*. These constructs will be formally defined and their (temporal) relationship will be specified in a set of axioms. The model developed will provide the basis for the specification of the reasoning behind communication that will be described in the next chapter.

3.4.2 Definition of the Main Reasoning Constructs

In the remainder of this chapter, we take the simple scenario of an agent x's attempt in delegating the achievement of one of his goals to another agent y, and an agent y's attempt in adopting the achievement of another agent's (here x's) goal. It is also important to note that hereafter, in all the formulae involving agents x and y, $y \neq x$.

The definitions given in this subsection make use of two important decision constructs: '*willing*' and '*want*'. These constructs correspond to the decisions to be made on the choices in an agent's desire-accessible worlds at a given time point. Desire-accessible worlds may be viewed as decision trees in classical decision theory [RG91b]. In a single-agent system these choices correspond to the choice of plans to achieve a certain end. We represent such decisions with the '*willing*' construct. For example, (Willing x φ) means that agent x is willing to achieve the state of affairs φ individually, that is, he has chosen a plan to achieve φ. In a multi-agent settings, other types of choices exist. Typically these choices correspond to an agent's chosen cooperating party. In the context of task delegation we require to represent an agent's chosen cooperating party who would be the actor of achieving the agent's desired end. This choice is represented by the '*want*' construct. For example, (Want x y φ) means that agent x has chosen agent y to achieve the state of affairs φ, in other words, it denotes x's final decision on the choice of agent. These constructs will not be formally defined in our general theory, since their truth or falsity should be evaluated by some deliberation procedures that need to be defined as part of the theory of the application in question. The important fact to note here is that these decisions are the links between an agents goals and the resulting intentions.

The following axioms are enforced on these decision constructs, to ensure that these decisions are made on formulae that an agent holds as a goal.

Axiom 8. (Willing y φ) $\Rightarrow$ (GOAL y E(Achieves y φ)).

Axiom 9. (Want x y φ) $\Rightarrow$ (GOAL x E(Achieves y φ)).

Furthermore, we require the following axiom to hold:

Axiom 10. (Want y y φ) $\Leftrightarrow$ (Willing y φ).

Finally the following abbreviation is used to express that an agent believes whether a formula is true or false, i.e., he holds a belief about the value of a formula [12]:

$$(\text{Aware } x\ \varphi) \stackrel{def}{=} (\text{BEL } x\ \varphi) \lor (\text{BEL } x\ \neg\varphi).$$

Having these constructs, we are in the position to define 'potential for cooperation' (PfC), 'pre-commitment' and 'commitment' of two agents. Since our theory takes an internal perspective, each of these constructs are defined once in the context of task delegation (agent x's perspective) and once in the context of task adoption (agent y's perspective). To distinguish the two, the corresponding operators have either the subscript 'd' (for delegation), or 'a' (for adoption).

Task Delegation

The formal definitions are provided in Figure 3.6. Informally:

- Agent $\underline{x}$ sees a *potential for cooperation* with agent $\underline{y}$ with respect to his goal state φ, such that y achieves at least ψ, if
  1. x has φ as a goal;
  2. x is not willing to achieve φ individually;
  3. x believes that one way of achieving φ is first to achieve ψ, and has ψ as a subgoal;[13]; and
  4. x has it as a goal that y achieves at least ψ.[14]
- Agent $\underline{x}$ is *pre-committed* to agent $\underline{y}$ such that y achieves φ, if
  1. x sees a potential for cooperation with y such that y achieves φ;[15] and
  2. x wants that y achieves φ.
     (Note that here, φ denotes the specific *term of cooperation* the agent is pre-committed to. This could be a goal, or a subgoal of higher level goal that had been previously negotiated upon).
- Agent $\underline{x}$ is *committed* to agent $\underline{y}$ achieving φ, means that:

---

[12] Aware is only an abbreviation, it is not to be confused with the general logics of 'awareness' in the literature, which involve logics of implicit and explicit beliefs (see [FH85]).

[13] Note that this belief is a logical consequence of the goal, based on the belief-goal compatibility axiom given in Section 3.3.4

[14] Note that here φ can be viewed as the context of negotiation, or the top-level goal, and ψ as x's current desired term of cooperation or in other words its current preference.

[15] The representation (PfC$_d$ x y φ) is used as a short form for (PfC$_d$ x y φ φ). Similarly for PfC$_a$.

$$(\text{PfC}_d\ x\ y\ \varphi\ \psi) \quad \overset{def}{=} \quad \left[\begin{array}{l} (\text{GOAL}\ x\ \text{E}\ \Diamond\ \varphi)\ \wedge \\ \neg(\text{Willing}\ y\ \varphi)\ \wedge \\ (\text{GOAL}\ x\ \text{E}(\psi\ B\ \varphi))\ \wedge \\ (\text{GOAL}\ x\ \text{E}(\text{Achieves}\ y\ \psi)) \end{array} \right].$$

$$(\text{Pre\_commit}_d\ x\ y\ \varphi) \quad \overset{def}{=} \quad \left[\begin{array}{l} (\text{PfC}_d\ x\ y\ \varphi)\ \wedge \\ (\text{Want}\ x\ y\ \varphi) \end{array} \right].$$

$$(\text{Commit}_d\ x\ y\ \varphi) \quad \overset{def}{=} \quad \left[\begin{array}{l} (\text{INTEND}\ x\ \text{E}(\text{Achieves}\ y\ \varphi)))\ \wedge \\ (\text{BEL}\ x\ \text{E}\ \Diamond\ (\text{INTEND}\ y\ \text{E}(\text{Achieves}\ y\ \varphi))) \end{array} \right].$$

Fig. 3.6. Task Delegation: Formal definitions of the Reasoning Constructs

1. x has committed to the choice of y achieving φ;
2. x believes that y will eventually commit to achieving φ.

Task Adoption

The formal definitions are provided in Figure 3.7 and defined informally as follows:

– Agent y sees a *potential for cooperation* with agent x with respect to a goal state φ, such that y achieves at least ψ, if
  1. y believes that x has it as a goal that y achieves φ; and
  2. y believes that one of the ways of achieving φ would be to first achieve ψ and has ψ as a subgoal, and
  3. y has it as a goal to achieve ψ, by carrying out some plan of actions.
– Agent y is *pre-committed* to agent x in achieving φ, if
  1. y sees a potential for cooperation with x such that y achieves φ; and
  2. y is willing to achieve φ.
– Agent y is *committed* to agent x in achieving φ, means that
  1. y intends to carry out a plan that would achieve φ; and
  2. y believes that x will eventually commit to the choice of y achieving φ.

Note that having a goal of achieving a state of affairs by carrying out a plan of actions, does not mean that the agent intends (or is committed) to the execution of that plan. Only if the agent is also '*willing*' to achieve the plan individually, does he intend or commit to the execution of the plan. In this sense, goals have instrumental functions and characterise but a partial commitment to a plan choice but not a full commitment.

Therefore, from detecting a potential for cooperation to making a commitment, the agents progressively have stronger beliefs about each others' attitude, and furthermore, have made stronger decisions about the possibility of engaging in a cooperation.

$$(\text{PfC}_a \; y \; x \; \varphi \; \psi) \quad \overset{def}{=} \quad \left[\begin{array}{l} (\text{BEL } y \; (\text{GOAL } x \; E \; \Diamond \; \varphi)) \; \wedge \\ (\text{GOAL } y \; E(\psi \; B \; \varphi)) \; \wedge \\ (\text{GOAL } y \; E(\text{Achieves } y \; \psi)) \end{array} \right] .$$

$$(\text{Pre\_commit}_a \; y \; x \; \varphi) \quad \overset{def}{=} \quad \left[\begin{array}{l} (\text{PfC}_a \; y \; x \; \varphi) \; \wedge \\ (\text{Willing } y \; \varphi) \end{array} \right] .$$

$$(\text{Commit}_a \; y \; x \; \varphi) \quad \overset{def}{=} \quad \left[\begin{array}{l} (\text{INTEND } y \; E(\text{Achieves } y \; \varphi)) \; \wedge \\ (\text{BEL } y \; E \; \Diamond \; (\text{INTEND } x \; E(\text{Achieves } y \; \varphi))) \end{array} \right] .$$

Fig. 3.7. Task Adoption: Formal definition of the Reasoning Constructs

3.4.3 Axioms of Pre-commitments and Commitments

The axioms introduced in this section are (temporal) restrictions enforced on the relationship between the three reasoning constructs defined in the previous subsection. These axioms are considered as the basic axioms of our theory.

Since we take an internal perspective the axioms and theorems that will be outlined throughout this section come in pairs once for task delegation and once for task adoption. But since they are very similar in each context, only the proof of theorems related to task delegation will be provided.

The first axioms of our theory are Axioms 11 and 12 which ensure that an agent does not make a pre-commitment on some terms of cooperation (here ψ, if he already believes that the other agent is not going to make a pre-commitment under those terms. Note that here it is a delicate difference between '*not being aware of the other agent's attitude*' and actually '*holding a belief about the status of the other agent's attitude*'.

Axiom 11. $(\text{BEL } x \; (\neg(\text{Pre\_commit}_a \; y \; x \; \psi)) \Rightarrow \neg(\text{Pre\_commit}_d \; x \; y \; \psi).$

Axiom 12. $(\text{BEL } x \; \neg(\text{Pre\_commit}_d \; x \; y \; \psi)) \Rightarrow \neg(\text{Pre\_commit}_a \; y \; x \; \psi).$

As was discussed earlier, the existing approaches to formalising joint commitments, rely on a recursive definition of mutual beliefs, where a group of agents are said to be jointly committed to cooperate in order to achieve a certain goal, if each group member is individually committed and believes that this commitment is mutual. For example for two agents x and y, according to these definitions, x is said to be committed if he believes that y is also committed, and believes that y believes that x is already committed and so on. Similarly for y. Such a definition however, does not provide us with any insights as how a group would indeed arrive at such shared mental states, since each agent would only make a commitment if he believes that the other has already made a commitment.

Our convention makes use of a weaker condition for forming an agent to agent commitment. It requires both agents to be *at least* pre-committed *before* any of them makes a commitment. This is captured in propositions 1 and 2, by which it is sufficient for an agent to be pre-committed and believe that the other agent is either pre-committed or is already committed, *before* he makes a full commitment[16].

Prop. 1.
$$\left[\begin{array}{l} (\text{Pre\_commit}_d \; x \; y \; \psi) \; \wedge \\ \left(\begin{array}{l} (\text{BEL} \; x \; (\text{Pre\_commit}_a \; y \; x \; \psi)) \; \vee \\ (\text{BEL} \; x \; (\text{Commit}_a \; y \; x \; \psi)) \end{array} \right) \end{array} \right] \Leftrightarrow \text{A} \bigcirc (\text{Commit}_d \; x \; y \; \psi).$$

Prop. 2.
$$\left[\begin{array}{l} (\text{Pre\_commit}_a \; y \; x \; \psi) \; \wedge \\ \left(\begin{array}{l} (\text{BEL} \; y \; (\text{Pre\_commit}_d \; x \; y \; \psi)) \; \vee \\ (\text{BEL} \; y \; (\text{Commit}_d \; x \; y \; \psi)) \end{array} \right) \end{array} \right] \Leftrightarrow \text{A} \bigcirc (\text{Commit}_a \; y \; x \; \psi).$$

For practical purposes, we also wish to express under which conditions an agent would *actively* not form a commitment or give up a commitment. Referring to propositions 1and 2, ideally, if in a given state the left hand side of the equivalence relation is not satisfied, the agent would not make a commitment in the next state, on *all*the paths emanating from that state. But these propositions only guarantee that at least for *some* path this would be the case. To be able to capture both the active formation and revision criteria, we first introduce the following abbreviation, (see also the next chapter):

$$p \longleftrightarrow q \stackrel{def}{=} (p \Leftrightarrow \text{A} \bigcirc q) \wedge (\neg p \Leftrightarrow \text{A} \neg \bigcirc q).$$

We call the left conjunct the *formation relation* and the right conjunct the *revision relation*. The above propositions can now be replaced by the following axioms which express both the formation and the revision conditions for agent to agent commitments.

Axiom 13.
$$\left[\begin{array}{l} (\text{Pre\_commit}_d \; x \; y \; \psi) \; \wedge \\ \left(\begin{array}{l} (\text{BEL} \; x \; (\text{Pre\_commit}_a \; y \; x \; \psi)) \; \vee \\ (\text{BEL} \; x \; (\text{Commit}_a \; y \; x \; \psi)) \end{array} \right) \end{array} \right] \longleftrightarrow (\text{Commit}_d \; x \; y \; \psi).$$

Axiom 14.
$$\left[\begin{array}{l} (\text{Pre\_commit}_a \; y \; x \; \psi) \; \wedge \\ \left(\begin{array}{l} (\text{BEL} \; y \; (\text{Pre\_commit}_d \; x \; y \; \psi)) \; \vee \\ (\text{BEL} \; y \; (\text{Commit}_d \; x \; y \; \psi)) \end{array} \right) \end{array} \right] \longleftrightarrow (\text{Commit}_a \; y \; x \; \psi).$$

Note that these two axioms are consistent with (though in virtue of the temporal relationship do not imply) the goal-intention compatibility axiom (Axiom 2 Section 3.3.4), that is:

(INTEND x E(Achieves y ψ)) $\Rightarrow$ (GOAL x E(Achieves y ψ)).
(INTEND y E(Achieves y ψ)) $\Rightarrow$ (GOAL y E(Achieves y ψ)).

---

[16] Note that in all the propositions and axioms that follow, φ and ψ are O-formulae, (see section 2.4.2 more details).

Since the agents obey the same convention, we make the following assumption:

Assumption 1: All the above axioms and subsequently their derivations are believed by the agents.

Having this assumption, we can now make some properties of the theory explicit. The most trivial, yet important property is expressed in the following theorems:

Theorem 3. (BEL x ¬(Pre_commit$_s$ y x ψ)) $\Rightarrow$ A¬ $\bigcirc$ (Commit$_d$ x y ψ).

Theorem 4. (BEL y ¬(Pre_commit$_d$ x y ψ)) $\Rightarrow$ A¬ $\bigcirc$ (Commit$_s$ y x ψ).

Proof: The proof directly follows from Axioms 11 and 13.

Therefore, if one of the agents in some way or another does not agree on participating in a certain terms of cooperation (here ψ), the other agent will no longer pursue on negotiating on those terms. Note once more that ψ may be the current terms of cooperation or an agent's current preference in the context of previously negotiated term (e.g., φ in the definitions). In this sense, these theorems only state that cooperating with respect to ψ is not agreed upon, but the negotiation could still proceed on a different term related to φ.

The following two theorems capture one of the important common intuitions regarding joint commitment, that is, whenever an agent comes to believe that the other agent is no longer committed, then he will also drop his commitment. Alternatively, an agent will not make a commitment in the future state, if he believes that the other agent will never make a commitment.

Theorem 5.

$$\left[\begin{array}{l} \text{(BEL } x \text{ (BEL } y \text{ (Pre\_commit}_d \; x \; y \; \psi))) \; \wedge \\ \text{(BEL } x \text{ A}\neg \Diamond \text{ (Commit}_s \; y \; x \; \psi) \end{array} \right] \Rightarrow \text{A}\neg \bigcirc \text{(Commit}_d \; x \; y \; \psi).$$

Theorem 6.

$$\left[\begin{array}{l} \text{(BEL } y \text{ (BEL } x \text{ (Pre\_commit}_s \; y \; x \; \psi))) \; \wedge \\ \text{(BEL } y \text{ A}\neg \Diamond \text{ (Commit}_d \; x \; y \; \psi)) \end{array} \right] \Rightarrow \text{A}\neg \bigcirc \text{(Commit}_s \; y \; x \; \psi).$$

Proof: The first step below results from the above assumption on the relationship between the temporal operators '$\Diamond$' and '$\bigcirc$'. The second step results from our assumption on Axiom 14. From these two steps the left hand side of our theory implies that agent y is no longer pre-committed (step 3) which then from Theorem 3 leads to A¬ $\bigcirc$ Commit$_d$.

1. (BEL x A¬ $\Diamond$ (Commit$_s$ y x ψ)) $\Rightarrow$ (BEL x A¬ $\bigcirc$ (Commit$_s$ y x ψ))

2.

$$\text{(BEL } x \text{ A}\neg \bigcirc \text{ (Commit}_s \; y \; x \; \psi)) \Rightarrow$$
$$\left[\begin{array}{l} \text{(BEL } x \text{ ¬(Pre\_commit}_s \; y \; x \; \psi)) \; \vee \\ \text{(BEL } x \left(\begin{array}{l} \text{¬(BEL } y \text{ (Pre\_commit}_d \; x \; y \; \psi) \; \wedge \\ \text{¬(BEL } y \text{ (Commit}_d \; x \; y \; \psi) \end{array} \right)) \end{array} \right]$$

3. $LHS \Rightarrow (\text{BEL } x \ \neg(\text{Pre\_commit}_s \ y \ x \ \psi))$.

□

An important aspect of our convention is that the agents should communicate certain beliefs so that they could become aware of each others attitudes towards a possible cooperation. One such requirement is that the first agent who makes a commitment must communicate this to the other agent. Since communication in the context of this work will be discussed in the next chapter, here we make the following assumption:

Assumption 2: If an agent has made a commitment then he believes that the other agent will eventually believe that he has made a commitment:

$\vdash (\text{Commit}_d \ x \ y \ \psi) \Rightarrow (\text{BEL } x \ A \Diamond (\text{BEL } y \ (\text{Commit}_d \ x \ y \ \psi)))$

$\vdash (\text{Commit}_s \ y \ x \ \psi) \Rightarrow (\text{BEL } y \ A \Diamond (\text{BEL } x \ (\text{Commit}_s \ y \ x \ \psi)))$

Intuitively, through communication agents revise their beliefs. Our next assumption is:

Assumption 3: An agent's belief about the status of pre-commitment of another agent changes only through communication.

For instance if an agent believes that the other agent is now pre-committed, this belief persists in the future states (until he receives a message from the other agent to the effect that this belief should no longer hold). To capture this assumption, we introduce the following axioms:

Axiom 15. $(\text{BEL } x \ (\text{Pre\_commit}_s \ y \ x \ \psi)) \Rightarrow (\text{BEL } x \ A \Box (\text{Pre\_commit}_s \ y \ x \ \psi))$.

Axiom 16. $(\text{BEL } x \ \neg(\text{Pre\_commit}_s \ y \ x \ \psi)) \Rightarrow (\text{BEL } x \ A \Box \neg(\text{Pre\_commit}_s \ y \ x \ \psi))$.

Axiom 17. $(\text{BEL } y \ (\text{Pre\_commit}_d \ x \ y \ \psi)) \Rightarrow (\text{BEL } y \ A \Box (\text{Pre\_commit}_d \ x \ y \ \psi))$.

Axiom 18. $(\text{BEL } y \ \neg(\text{Pre\_commit}_d \ x \ y \ \psi)) \Rightarrow (\text{BEL } y \ A \Box \neg(\text{Pre\_commit}_d \ x \ y \ \psi))$.

Note that in our modelling of beliefs, an agent's belief may change in another time point. For instance if x believes now that y is pre-committed, from the above axioms, it is in the current state that he believes y will remain pre-committed. But since beliefs can change with time, it is perfectly acceptable for an agent to believe at the next time point (through communication) that y is no longer pre-committed.

Now it is possible to show that if an agent has made a commitment and still believes that the other agent is pre-committed, then he believes that eventually the other agent will also make a commitment. This is stated in the following theorems:

Theorem 7.

$$\left[\begin{array}{l} (\text{Commit}_d \ x \ y \ \psi) \ \wedge \\ (\text{BEL } x \ (\text{Pre\_commit}_s \ y \ x \ \psi)) \end{array} \right] \Rightarrow (\text{BEL } x \ A \Diamond (\text{Commit}_s \ y \ x \ \psi)).$$

Theorem 8.

$$\left[\begin{array}{l} (\text{Commit}_a \; y \; x \; \psi) \; \wedge \\ (\text{BEL} \; y \; (\text{Pre\_commit}_d \; x \; y \; \psi)) \end{array} \right] \Rightarrow (\text{BEL} \; y \; A \; \lozenge \; (\text{Commit}_d \; x \; y \; \psi)).$$

Proof: The first step results from the temporal implication: $\text{Commit}_d \Rightarrow A \lozenge \text{Commit}_d$, and assumption 2 above. The second step results from Axiom 15 and the third step from the temporal implication: $\Box p \Rightarrow \lozenge p$. From the above two steps the left hand side of the theorem implies the formula presented in the fourth step. Finally, the last step results from assumption 1 on Axiom 14.

1. $A \lozenge (\text{Commit}_d \; x \; y \; \psi) \Rightarrow (\text{BEL} \; x \; A \lozenge (\text{BEL} \; y \; (\text{Commit}_d \; x \; y \; \psi))$
2. $(\text{BEL} \; x \; (\text{Pre\_commit}_a \; y \; x \; \psi)) \Rightarrow (\text{BEL} \; x \; A \Box (\text{Pre\_commit}_a \; y \; x \; \psi))$
3. $\Rightarrow (\text{BEL} \; x \; A \lozenge (\text{Pre\_commit}_a \; y \; x \; \psi))$
4. $LHS \Rightarrow (\text{BEL} \; x \; A \lozenge (\text{BEL} \; y \; (\text{Commit}_d \; x \; y \; \psi)) \wedge (\text{Pre\_commit}_a \; y \; x \; \psi))$
5. $\Rightarrow (\text{BEL} \; x \; A \lozenge (\text{Commit}_a \; y \; x \; \psi)). \; \Box$

Another important intuition regarding joint commitment is that the acting agents start their cooperative activities only after they have made a joint commitment. The theory presented here captures this requirement since the acting agent (i.e. agent y) forms the intention to act towards the goal only after he has made a commitment to agent x, (see the definition of Commit_a).

Finally it is worth mentioning that this theory avoids the following problem: If agent y has adopted a goal and has made a commitment to agent x with respect to this goal, he will not attempt to delegate the achievement of the goal back to agent x. This is because in order for agent y to maintain his commitment he has to believe that agent x is pre-committed, and consequently believe that agent x sees a potential for cooperation. From the definition of potential for cooperation in the context of task delegation, y also can conclude that x is not '*willing*' to achieve that goal, and as a result will not adopt the goal. This is formally represented in the following steps:

1. $A \bigcirc (\text{Commit}_a \; y \; x \; \psi) \Rightarrow (\text{BEL} \; y \; (\text{Pre\_commit}_d \; x \; y \; \psi))$
2. $\Rightarrow (\text{BEL} \; y \; (\text{PfC}_d \; x \; y \; \psi))$
3. $\Rightarrow (\text{BEL} \; y \; \neg (\text{Willing} \; x \; \psi))$
4. $\Rightarrow (\text{BEL} \; y \; \neg (\text{PfC}_a \; y \; x \; \psi))$
5. $\Rightarrow \neg (\text{PfC}_d \; y \; x \; \psi)$

The following summarises some of the properties of joint commitments captured in this theory:

1. **(Formation conditions:)** An agent will make a commitment to another agent only if he has made a pre-commitment and believes that the other agent is either at least pre-committed or that the other agent is already committed, (Axioms 13 and 14).
2. At any stage during the negotiation, if an agent comes to believe that the other agent is not prepared to cooperate on the terms negotiated upon, the agent will not pursue negotiating on those terms any further and consequently will not make a commitment on those terms, (Theorems 3 and 4).

3. (**Revision conditions:**) If an agent is precommitted (or even already committed) to the other agent, but comes to know that the other agent has given up his commitment, or that the other agent will not make a commitment on those terms in the future, then the agent will also give up his commitment (Theorems 5 and 6).

4. If an agent makes a commitment to another agent, he believes that the other agent is already committed or will make a commitment, (Theorems 7 and 8). This is important, since it ensures that the state of joint-commitment will be reached.

5. The acting agent will start acting towards the joint goal, only after the joint commitment is established, (from the definition of Commit$_a$ and Theorem 4).

6. After making a commitment, the acting agent will not attempt to delegate the achievement of the joint goal back to the delegating agent.

The convention introduced is aimed to (i) guide the process of reasoning about cooperation, and (ii) guide certain belief maintenance and belief revisions in this process. In the theory presented here however, only the former is captured, taking the belief maintenance and revision for granted in Assumptions 2 and 3. In the next chapter, the focus is diverted to the latter by specifying the conditions under which agents must communicate certain new status regarding their current attitude towards a cooperation. The idea is therefore, to relax these assumptions by virtue of successful communication that is guided by the convention adopted.

3.5 Discussion

This chapter introduced our formal framework and argued that formalising mental attitudes with internal theories brings more insights into the practical aspects of the cognitive processes of agents.

The theory developed in this chapter is based on the BDI model of Rao and Georgeff, adopting their axioms and semantic constraints to relate the static interaction between these attitudes. One advantage of this model is that it captures many philosophical understandings of intentions. Furthermore, as will be demonstrated in the next chapter, modelling of these attitudes in terms of branching worlds enables us to draw parallels with the decision trees in decision theory and therefore identify how such theoretical models can be used to specify the reasoning processes of agents. For this purpose, two important decision constructs were identified, namely '*willing*' and '*want*' to respectively represent an agents choice to achieve a task individually, and an agent's choice to delegate a task to another agent. These constructs therefore characterise the decisions to be made in the process of means-end reasoning. Basically, it is the lack of such decision constructs that limits the practicality of the existing approaches.

This chapter also argued for a more practical modelling of joint attitudes by outlining a convention that does not rely on the recursive definition of mutual beliefs which are in practice hard or even impossible to establish. The convention outlined, identified three important reasoning constructs, namely, *potential for cooperation*, *pre-commitments* and agent to agent *commitments*, which respectively initiate a negotiation process in order to arrive at a mutual agreement, finalise the negotiation process and prompt the negotiating parties for a commitment, and finally initiate the cooperative activity.

In our theory, these constructs were defined in terms of beliefs, goals and intentions of individual agents and the decision constructs mentioned earlier. Based on the convention, agents make and maintain their commitment to one another as long as each is pre-committed and believes that the other agent is at least pre-committed. This intuition is captured in a pair of basic axioms (Axioms 13 and 14) which express the temporal relationship between agent to agent commitments and their maintenance conditions.

The theory presented in this chapter basically specified the conditions for commitment formation, maintenance and revision. Based on this theory and the convention introduced, the next chapter will provide the specification of the means-end reasoning process of an agent and demonstrate how communication arises from various possible states.

4. Specification of Reasoning behind Interactions

4.1 Overview

This chapter presents the specification of the means-end reasoning processes of agents in the context of individual task achievement, task delegation and task adoption. During this process an agent not only reasons about how to achieve a certain goal state, but also how to achieve sub-goals that arise as a result of reasoning about the means of achieving that goal. The goals to communicate are examples of sub-goals that may be formed during this process. As was discussed in the previous chapter, in order to cooperate, the agents need to agree on the terms of cooperation and make a commitment to one another. In this context, communication occurs in order to initiate a state of belief about a potential for a cooperation, to negotiate in order to arrive at an agreement on the terms of cooperation, and if as a result of negotiation an agreement is reached make a commitment on the agreed terms.

This chapter will first specify the formation and revision conditions for individual and agent to agent commitments in Section 4.3. Section 4.4 will then specify the reasoning states which lead to goals to communicate with the initial purpose of arriving at a state in which both agents have made a commitment. Section 4.5 will describe how appropriate communication plans may be selected during the means-end reasoning process to fulfill such goals. To bring the whole picture together, Section 4.6 will illustrate the process of means-end reasoning to engage in a potential cooperation by means of an example scenario. Finally, Section 4.7 will provide a summary and a discussion on this chapter.

4.2 Background

In the last chapter, the axioms of the theory specified the static interactions between the mental attitudes of beliefs, goals and intentions and specified the temporal relationship between pre-commitments and commitments. Based on this theory, this chapter aims at specifying the reasoning process by ensuring progress from a current reasoning state to future states consistent with the models of our theory.

Hence, the means-end reasoning process is modelled as reasoning state transitions. These transitions are specified in a set of rules. According to the conditions that hold in a given state, these rules specify the next valid state to which the transition must proceed. Since this process is a temporal state transition, these rules are comparable to the temporal logic specification of *liveness properties*[1] of concurrent programs [Pnu77], [Eme90]. In particular, the *temporal implication* which is of the form $\Box(\varphi \Rightarrow \Diamond\psi)$, where φ and ψ are past formulas, meaning that always if φ holds then eventually ψ will hold.

The specification rules employed here are somewhat different from the temporal implication. A rule $\varphi \longleftrightarrow \psi$ is defined to be:

$$\varphi \longleftrightarrow \psi \overset{def}{=} \Box(\varphi \Leftrightarrow \mathsf{A} \bigcirc \psi).$$

The reason for this difference is that these rules not only need to specify the formation of commitments and goals that lead to communication, but also their maintenance and revision conditions. Therefore a rule $\varphi \longleftrightarrow \psi$ means that ψ is formed and maintained as long as φ holds, and whenever φ does not hold, ψ will not hold in the next state. This will be discussed in greater detail in the next section.

4.3 Rules of Commitments

This section outlines the rules for formation of various types of commitments, namely, individual intentions (in individual task achievement), and agent-agent commitments to delegate or adopt a task. An agent forms an *intention to act* either towards one of his own goals or towards an adopted goal. We require that an intention towards an adopted goal to be formed only after both agents have agreed to cooperate. As a result, such an intention is formed only after the acting agent has made a commitment (i.e., Commit$_a$) to the other agent. But, we still require to state under what conditions an agent forms an intention towards achievement of one of his own goals. These conditions are captured in the first rule in Figure 4.1. Since according to our theory, intentions to act directly lead to execution of the intended plans, the first condition in this rule avoids situations in which an agent has made a pre-commitment but does not as yet know whether the other agent also agrees to his terms. As mentioned above, the intention in the context of task adoption should be formed only after the agents have made a commitment to one another. The other two conditions in this rule basically captures the intuition that *intentions are chosen desired paths to achieve some desired ends*.

The conditions for formation, maintenance and revision of agent-agent commitments are directly taken from Axiom 13 and Axiom 14 respectively, and the corresponding rules are represented in Figure 4.1. Note that since

---

[1] Sometimes known as *progress properties*.

$$\forall x . (x \neq y) \wedge$$
$$\begin{bmatrix} \neg(\text{Pre\_commit}_{s} \ y \ x \ \varphi) \wedge \\ (\text{GOAL} \ y \ \text{E}(\text{Achieves} \ y \ \varphi)) \wedge \\ (\text{Willing} \ y \ \varphi) \end{bmatrix} \longleftrightarrow (\text{INTEND} \ y \ \text{E}(\text{Achieves} \ y \ \varphi)).$$

$$\begin{bmatrix} (\text{Pre\_commit}_{d} \ x \ y \ \varphi) \wedge \\ \left(\begin{array}{l} (\text{BEL} \ x \ (\text{Pre\_commit}_{s} \ y \ x \ \varphi)) \vee \\ (\text{BEL} \ x \ (\text{Commit}_{s} \ y \ x \ \varphi)) \end{array} \right) \end{bmatrix} \longleftrightarrow (\text{Commit}_{d} \ x \ y \ \varphi).$$

$$\begin{bmatrix} (\text{Pre\_commit}_{s} \ y \ x \ \varphi) \wedge \\ \left(\begin{array}{l} (\text{BEL} \ y \ (\text{Pre\_commit}_{d} \ x \ y \ \varphi)) \vee \\ (\text{BEL} \ y \ (\text{Commit}_{d} \ x \ y \ \varphi)) \end{array} \right) \end{bmatrix} \longleftrightarrow (\text{Commit}_{s} \ y \ x \ \varphi).$$

Fig. 4.1. Commitment Formation Rules

these rules express an equivalence relation between the conditions that hold in the current state and the conditions that should hold in the next state, whenever one of the conditions in the left hand side of the rule no longer holds then in the next state the agent should drop his commitment. For instance, if agent x no longer wishes to pursue his goal, or that he comes to believe that the other agent is no longer committed, he will give up his commitment to that goal.

Hence, specification of the commitment formation, maintenance and revision conditions directly map to the axioms of our theory. Having outlined the commitment rules, next section outlines the rules for formation of goals that lead to communication.

4.4 Rules of Goals to Communicate

By communication agents can update their belief about whether, when and how they wish to cooperate. The need to communicate arises during the means-end reasoning process to achieve a certain goal. These needs are in fact subgoals that are produced dynamically which like other goals are fed back into the means-end reasoning process to find appropriate communication plans that would fulfill them.

Hence, we require to specify what conditions should hold in a reasoning state in order for the reasoning process to proceed to the future states in which these goals are formed and later satisfied by appropriate communication plans. To characterise these reasoning states, we base our specification within the framework of the convention described in the previous chapter, Section 3.4.1. According to this convention, (roughly) communication takes place in the following situations:

1. when an agent has detected a potential for cooperation, but does not have enough information about the other agent's attitude towards this possibility;

2. when an agent has made the final decision on the terms he agrees to cooperate on (i.e., he has made a pre-commitment), and requires to know if the other agent will also agree on his suggested terms;

3. when an agent agrees with the other agent's suggested terms and makes a commitment; and

4. when an agent is aware of the other agent's interest for a cooperation but does not wish to participate, or cooperate under the already negotiated terms.

Having these rough descriptions, next we discuss how these conditions are formalised. An agent's goal to communicate is directed towards two objectives: (i) update of the other agent's belief, that is, the fact that the agent wishes to convey to the other agent about his own attitude; and (ii) update of his own belief about the other agent's attitude. Having in mind that we take an internal perspective, for an agent z, let ρ denote the first objective and (Does $z\ \gamma$?) the second objective[2]. Then a goal to communicate is expressed as follows:

$$(\text{GOAL } z \text{ E } \Diamond\ \delta), \text{ where } \delta = \rho\ \wedge\ (\text{Does } z\ \gamma?).$$

Each specific goal to communicate is expressed by (GOAL z E $\Diamond\ \delta_i$), where z denotes agent x in the context of task delegation, and agent y in the context of task adoption. Furthermore, each δ_i expresses each specific objective that the agent desires to fulfill.

As with the specification of formation of commitments, formation of these goals are specified by a set of rules of the form ($\varphi\ \longleftrightarrow\ \psi$), where the left hand side of the rule specifies the conditions that must hold in the current reasoning state and the right hand side of the rule specifies the condition that must hold in the future state (here, the specific communication goal). These rules[3] are presented in Figure 4.2 and Figure 4.3.

It is important to note that although the conditions related to the rules for task delegation are similar to those related to task adoption, they are *formally* not identical. In other words, a rule in each context leads to a different goal and different communication plan that fulfills that goal.

The conditions for formation of goals to communicate will be discussed in detail next.

---

[2] Having the goal of (Does $z\ \gamma$?), expresses the fact that agent z has it as a goal to execute a plan in order to find out if γ (here, a fact about the other agent's attitude) holds. (see Section 3.3.3 for the semantics.)

[3] Due to space restrictions, the right hand side of the rules, (i.e., the corresponding (GOAL z E $\Diamond\ \delta_i$)) are omitted in the figures and only the particular ρ_i and γ_i are defined.

Rule 1: If an agent

1. has detected a potential for cooperation with respect to a goal φ and his preference ψ (i.e., his preferred terms); but
2. has not as yet made a decision on the final terms, (for instance he cannot or does not wish to make a decision before he obtains more information about the other agent);
3. does not hold any belief about whether the other agent agrees that this potential exists, and
4. believes that the other agent is not aware[4] of his particular interest for a cooperation,

then he will form the goal of communicating his interest for cooperation to the other agent and becoming aware of the other agent's attitude towards this possibility. Such states may lead to negotiation in order to arrive at some agreed terms of cooperation.

Note that if the agent is aware of the other agent's attitude towards this possibility, then he must make a decision on some other (more preferred) terms, or else make a pre-commitment with respect to the negotiated terms (see below).

Rule 2: If an agent

1. has made his final decision on some terms he agrees to cooperate (i.e., has made a pre-commitment); but
2. does not know if these terms are also agreed by the other agent (i.e., whether the other agent will make a commitment); and
3. believes that the other agent is not aware of his decision,

then he will form the goal to communicate his agreed terms to the other agent and find out whether the other agent also agrees with these terms.

Rule 3: If an agent

1. has made a commitment; and
2. believes that the other agent is not aware of his commitment,

then he will form the goal of letting his commitment known to the other agent.

Note that according to our theory, when an agent makes a commitment, he believes that the other agent is either already committed or will eventually become committed.

---

[4] Reminder: (Aware $z\ \varphi$) $\overset{def}{=}$ (BEL $z\ \varphi$) $\vee$ (BEL $z\ \neg\varphi$)

Rules	Task Delegation
1	$\left[\begin{array}{l}(\mathsf{PfC_d}\ x\ y\ \varphi\ \psi)\ \wedge \\ \neg(\mathsf{Pre\_commit_d}\ x\ y\ (\varphi \vee \psi))\ \wedge \\ \neg(\mathsf{Aware}\ x\ (\mathsf{PfC_a}\ y\ x\ \varphi\ \psi))\ \wedge \\ (\mathsf{BEL}\ x\ \neg(\mathsf{Aware}\ y\ (\mathsf{PfC_d}\ x\ y\ \varphi\ \psi)))\end{array}\right]$ $\rho_1 = (\mathsf{BEL}\ y\ (\mathsf{PfC_d}\ x\ y\ \varphi\ \psi))\quad \gamma_1 = (\mathsf{PfC_a}\ y\ x\ \varphi\ \psi)$
2	$\left[\begin{array}{l}(\mathsf{Pre\_commit_d}\ x\ y\ \psi)\ \wedge \\ \neg(\mathsf{Aware}\ x\ (\mathsf{Pre\_commit_a}\ y\ x\ \psi))\ \wedge \\ (\mathsf{BEL}\ x\ \neg(\mathsf{Aware}\ y\ (\mathsf{Pre\_commit_d}\ x\ y\ \psi)))\end{array}\right]$ $\rho_2 = (\mathsf{BEL}\ y\ (\mathsf{Pre\_commit_d}\ x\ y\ \psi))\quad \gamma_2 = (\mathsf{Pre\_commit_a}\ y\ x\ \psi)$
3	$\left[\begin{array}{l}(\mathsf{Commit_d}\ x\ y\ \varphi)\ \wedge \\ (\mathsf{BEL}\ x\ \neg(\mathsf{Aware}\ y\ (\mathsf{Commit_d}\ x\ y\ \psi)))\end{array}\right]$ $\rho_3 = (\mathsf{BEL}\ y\ (\mathsf{Commit_d}\ x\ y\ \psi))\quad \gamma_3 = \text{true}$
4	$\left[\begin{array}{l}(\mathsf{BEL}\ x\ (\mathsf{PfC_a}\ y\ x\ \varphi\ \psi))\ \wedge \\ \neg(\mathsf{Pre\_commit_d}\ x\ y\ \psi)\ \wedge \\ (\mathsf{BEL}\ x\ \neg(\mathsf{Aware}\ y\ \neg(\mathsf{Pre\_commit_d}\ x\ y\ \psi)))\end{array}\right]$ $\rho_4 = (\mathsf{BEL}\ y\ \neg(\mathsf{Pre\_commit_d}\ x\ y\ \psi))\quad \gamma_4 = \text{true}$

Fig. 4.2. Communciation Rules: Task Delegation

Rule 4: If an agent

1. believes that another agent is interested in his cooperation with respect to a goal φ and some preferred terms ψ, but
2. he does not wish or cannot participate in cooperating under those terms (i.e., ψ); and
3. believes that the other agent is not aware of this fact,

then he will form the goal of letting this fact known to the other agent.

Note that the condition $\neg(\mathsf{PfC_d}\ x\ y\ \psi)$ captures the *"lack of mutual interest in any terms of cooperation"* with respect to the terms ψ, since according to Theorem 3 and Theorem 4 in Section 3.4.3 in the previous chapter:

$$(\mathsf{BEL}\ x\ \neg(\mathsf{PfC_a}\ y\ x\ \psi)) \Rightarrow \neg(\mathsf{PfC_d}\ x\ y\ \psi)$$

Rules	Task Adoption
1	$\left[\begin{array}{l} (\text{PfC}_a \ y \ x \ \varphi \ \psi) \wedge \\ \neg(\text{Pre\_commit}_a \ y \ x \ (\varphi \vee \psi)) \wedge \\ \neg(\text{Aware} \ y \ (\text{PfC}_d \ x \ y \ \varphi \ \psi)) \wedge \\ (\text{BEL} \ y \ \neg(\text{Aware} \ x \ (\text{PfC}_a \ y \ x \ \varphi \ \psi))) \end{array}\right]$ $\rho_5 = (\text{BEL} \ x \ (\text{PfC}_a \ y \ x \ \varphi \ \psi)) \quad \gamma_5 = (\text{PfC}_d \ x \ y \ \varphi \ \psi)$
2	$\left[\begin{array}{l} (\text{Pre\_commit}_a \ y \ x \ \psi) \wedge \\ \neg(\text{Aware} \ y \ (\text{Pre\_commit}_d \ x \ y \ \psi)) \wedge \\ (\text{BEL} \ y \ \neg(\text{Aware} \ x \ (\text{Pre\_commit}_a \ y \ x \ \psi))) \end{array}\right]$ $\rho_6 = (\text{BEL} \ x \ (\text{Pre\_commit}_a \ y \ x \ \psi)) \quad \gamma_6 = (\text{Pre\_commit}_d \ x \ y \ \psi)$
3	$\left[\begin{array}{l} (\text{Commit}_a \ y \ x \ \psi) \wedge \\ (\text{BEL} \ y \ \neg(\text{Aware} \ x \ (\text{Commit}_a \ y \ x \ \psi))) \end{array}\right]$ $\rho_7 = (\text{BEL} \ x \ (\text{Commit}_a \ y \ x \ \psi)) \quad \gamma_7 = \text{true}$
4	$\left[\begin{array}{l} (\text{BEL} \ y \ (\text{PfC}_d \ x \ y \ \psi)) \wedge \\ (\neg(\text{Pre\_commit}_a \ y \ x \ \psi) \wedge \\ (\text{BEL} \ y \ \neg(\text{Aware} \ x \ \neg(\text{Pre\_commit}_a \ y \ x \ \psi)))) \end{array}\right]$ $\rho_8 = (\text{BEL} \ y \ \neg(\text{Pre\_commit}_a \ y \ x \ \psi))$ $\gamma_8 = \text{true}$
5	$\left[\begin{array}{l} (\text{Commit}_a \ y \ x \ \psi) \wedge \\ (\text{Aware} \ x \ (\text{Achieved} \ y \ \psi)) \wedge \\ (\text{BEL} \ y \ \neg(\text{Aware} \ x \ (\text{Achieved} \ y \ \psi))) \end{array}\right]$ *if* $(\text{BEL} \ y \ (\text{Achieved} \ y \ \psi))$ $\qquad\qquad\quad$ *then* $\rho_9 = (\text{BEL} \ x \ (\text{Achieved} \ y \ \psi))$, *elseif* $(\text{BEL} \ y \ \neg(\text{Achieved} \ y \ \psi))$ $\qquad\qquad\quad$ *then* $\rho_9 = (\text{BEL} \ x \ \neg(\text{Achieved} \ y \ \psi))$ $\gamma_9 = \text{true}$

Fig. 4.3. Communication Rules: Task Adoption

In other words, if agent x had been originally interested in some terms of cooperation and later finds out that the other agent was not, then he comes to believe that there is no potential for cooperation under those terms.

Finally, as can be seen in Figure 4.3, in the context of task adoption there is an additional rule (rule 5), which is not necessary, but can be added to the list of rules to ensure that once agent y has achieved the joint goal (or in our internal theory, the adopted goal), then he must let the status of success or failure of achievement of the goal be known to agent x.

Note that since these rules denote an equivalence relation between the conditions in two consecutive states, they also capture the maintenance and revision conditions of such goals. For instance if the communication has taken place and the goal is satisfied, at least one of the conditions towards mainte-nance of the goal no longer holds, and therefore the goal will be given up. For example consider rule 3 in the context of task delegation. After a successful communication, the condition (BEL x ¬(Aware y (Commit$_d$ x y ψ))) would no longer hold, and therefore x will no longer have the goal of making his commitment known to the other agent.

Having determined how goals are formed within the framework of our convention, next section describes how appropriate communication plans are chosen in order to achieve such goals.

4.5 Communication for a Potential Cooperation

The previous section described under what conditions certain goals to com-municate are formed. Such goals are considered as subgoals that are formed dynamically during the means-end reasoning process to achieve a higher-level goal. Like any other goal such subgoals are fed back into the means-end reasoning process to find the appropriate plans that satisfy them. In this case, these are a set of communication plans. To describe how these plans are selected in this process, first a number of communication plans will be described.

In principle, each agent is assumed to have two types of communicative actions: '$send(msg)$' and '$receive(msg)$'. The syntax and semantics of messages was given in the previous chapter in Sections 3.3.1 and 3.3.2. As a reminder, the set of messages MSG is given by:

$$MSG = MT \times U_{Ag} \times U_{Ag} \times \text{wff}(\mathcal{L}')$$

Informally, a message consists of a message type, a sender, a receiver and a well-formed formula of some communication language $\mathcal{L}'$ to express the actual "content" of the message. The role of message types is to convey the illocutionary force of a message that was discussed in chapter 2, Section 2.7. Roughly, a message type is used to convey the purpose of the message sent. For instance an '$inform$' message type conveys that the content of a message is an information that may be useful to the receiving agent, and a '$query$'

conveys that the message sent is a query that requires receiver's response. For the purpose of this thesis, the set of message types are restricted to the following:

$$MT = \{ \quad inform, \ query, \ reject, \\ demand, \ command, \ request, \\ offer, \ accept, \ propose, \ report\}$$

As will be seen later, the illocutionary force that is intended by each message type is conveyed by adoption of a specific communication goal described in the previous section. In other words, the conditions specified for adoption of each goal are in effect the semantics of a specific speech act.

Our framework admits only two types of *primitive communication plans* from which more complex plans may be constructed. A primitive communication plan may be any of the following plan expressions:

1. $\{send(msg)\}$
2. $\{send(msg_1) \ ; \ wait \ ; \ receive(msg_2)\}$

In the convention used in this book, primitive communication plans are distinguished by the message types of the message to be sent as a result of executing that plan. For instance, if the message type of the message to be sent as the first action of a plan is '*request*', then the primitive plan is also called a *request* plan.

As was discussed in the previous section, an agent's goal to communicate is directed towards two objectives: (i) update of the other agent's belief, that is, the fact that the sender wishes to convey to the receiver about his own attitude; and (ii) update of his own belief about the other agent's (i.e., the receiver's) attitude. For each specific goal, these two objectives were denoted by ρ_i and (**Does** $z \ \gamma_i$?), respectively.

Hence, to achieve a communication goal where $\gamma =$ **true**, the selected communication plan would solely consist of a 'send' action. Otherwise, the plan expression is of the latter form shown above, which means that the agent requires a response in order to update his own belief about the receiver's attitude.

Each specific goal described in the previous section may be satisfied by successful execution of at least one plan. For simplicity, in this work we assume that for each specific goal there is one and only one primitive communication plan that if executed successfully would achieve that goal[5]. This association is represented in the following table:

From the table above, and the rules presented in Figures 4.2 and 4.3 in the previous section, roughly, a *request* or a *propose* plan is executed when an agent sees a potential for cooperation but wishes to negotiate on the

---

[5] Otherwise, like other goals the agent has to deliberate and choose one of the plans. Also note that during the means-end reasoning process we assume that an agent has no other goals to choose from.

Table 4.1. Semantics of primitive communication plans

Task delegation			
Request δ_1	Demand δ_2	Command δ_3	Reject δ_4

Task adoption				
Propose δ_5	Offer δ_6	Accept δ_7	Reject δ_8	Report δ_9

terms, a *demand* or an *offer* plan is executed after an agent has made a pre-commitment with the purpose of prompting the receiver for a commitment, a *command* or an *accept* plan is executed after an agent has made a commitment, a *reject* plan is executed when the agent does not wish to participate in a cooperation, and a *report* plan is executed after the acting agent has acted towards the joint goal and must let the status of achievement of the goal be known to the other agent.

As was mentioned earlier, the actual content of a message is a well-formed formula of some communication language $\mathcal{L}'$. The minimum requirement is that the content of the message sent as a result of executing a communication plan, reflects the specific information that the agent is aiming the receiver to believe (i.e., (GOAL x E $\Diamond$ ρ_i)). For instance if agent x has made a pre-commitment and as a result has the goal (GOAL x E $\Diamond$ ρ_2), the content of the message to be sent by executing a *demand* plan must reflect (Pre_commit$_d$ x y φ).

There are a number of assumptions that we make about these plans:

1. After receiving a message, the receiving agent believes the 'content' of the message (i.e. from the content of the message received, the agent concludes the corresponding ρ_i). For instance, if agent y receives a demand from agent x, then according to this assumption, ρ_2 will hold, that is, y's belief will be updated such that now (BEL y (Pre_commit$_d$ x y φ)) holds.
2. After sending a message, the sending agent believes that the receiving agent has received the message and that the sending agent believes that the receiving agent believes the 'content' of the message.

These assumptions are captured in the following axiom, where p_i is any communication plan:

Axiom 19. A $\Box$ [(Succeeded z p_i) $\Rightarrow$ ((BEL z ρ_i) $\wedge$ (Aware z γ_i))].

If we also assume that execution of a communication plan is always successful, then due to this axiom the second assumption in Section 3.4.3 in the previous chapter would be a theorem in our theory, that is:

Theorem 9. $\vdash$ A $\Diamond$ Commit$_d$ $\Rightarrow$ (BEL x A $\Diamond$ (BEL y Commit$_d$)).

Theorem 10. $\vdash A \Diamond \text{Commit}_a \Rightarrow (\text{BEL } y \, A \Diamond (\text{BEL } x \, \text{Commit}_a))$.

The proof is trivial: The first agent who makes a commitment, will form the goal of letting the other agent know that he has made a commitment. As a result of this goal he will execute a *command* plan (or an *accept* plan according to the perspective). Since we assume that the execution of such plans are always successful, from the above axiom, the other agent will believe that the (first) agent has made a commitment. Since all this occurs during a time period, from the necessitation rule on beliefs, it can be proved that the (first) agent believes that the other agent will eventually believe that he has made a commitment.

Since we make the assumption that an agent has one and only one communication plan in his plan library that achieves a specific communication goal, the process of means-end reasoning to achieve such goals is very trivial. In effect, because of this assumption we can conclude:

$$(\text{GOAL } z \, E \Diamond \, \delta_i) \;\Rightarrow A \Diamond (\text{INTEND } z \, E \Diamond \, \delta_i)$$
$$\Rightarrow A \Diamond (\text{INTEND } z \, E \Diamond \, (\text{Does } z \, p_i)).$$

If we do not make this assumption, then the agent must deliberate and find the most appropriate plan. In which case the means-end reasoning for such goals is the same as that for the other types of goals. For instance the agent may deliberate whether he wishes to communicate directly with the other agent or communicate indirectly via a third party.

During the negotiation phase the agents may require to acquire some information before making a particular proposal. These are in general made by a '*query*' plan. Similarly the agents may simple provide further information as supplements. In this case the '*inform*' plan may be executed. If for instance at some point one of the agents drops his commitment and the convention requires that he communicates this to the other agent, then this fact will be communicated by executing an inform plan. The specification of the goals that lead to execution of these plans are not considered in this work.

Having defined how the goals to communicate are formed and how appropriate communication plans may be selected in order to achieve such goals, next section demonstrates the whole concept by means of an example scenario.

4.6 Illustration

The previous sections specified in the context of task delegation and task adoption how various types of commitments and certain goals to communicate are formed. Further, it was described how such goals are satisfied by successful execution of appropriate communication plans. This section aims to bring the whole picture together by demonstrating how the theory developed in the previous chapter and the specification given so far meets our convention and consequently demonstrate how the process of means-end reasoning to delegate or adopt a task takes place.

For this purpose, an example scenario in road transportation and shipping domain is chosen. The shipping company considered, has a number of trucks and a number of employees: a coordinator and truck drivers. The coordinator's task is to distribute and allocate customer orders to the trucks while minimising the costs. In some occasions the company also makes contracts with private sub-contractors. Although satisfying orders by contracting out to sub-contractors usually cost the company more than allocating orders to the company's own transporters, in some occasions the company needs to contract out to meet the customer demands.

The particular scenario we will be looking at is one where the coordinator has received some orders to be transported to a particular destination, from that destination some other orders transported to other destinations in that vicinity and finally some orders picked up from there and returned to the customer's base. The coordinator's main goal is to satisfy all these orders as demanded by the customer. This as well as the costs need to be negotiated upon with the (potential) sub-contractor(s). Let the coordinator be represented by agent x, the sub-contractor by agent y, and formulae φ, ψ and ψ' represent the following transport orders, where $O_{i,j}$ represents orders to be transported from destination i to destination j.

φ (transport $O_{0,1} \wedge O_{1,2} \wedge O_{2,3} \wedge O_{3,2} \wedge O_{2,0}$)
ψ (transport $O_{0,1} \wedge O_{2,0}$)
ψ' (transport $O_{0,1} \wedge O_{1,2} \wedge O_{2,0}$)

Within the framework of the model of cooperation considered in this work, the coordinator sees a potential for cooperation with the sub-contractor, with respect to the overall goal of transporting all the aforementioned orders as demanded by the customer. Let this goal be denoted by φ. His initial preference at the current stage is also all the orders denoted by φ. But the coordinator needs first to negotiate these terms with the sub-contractor in order to come to some sort of agreement. This (first) state is shown in Figure 4.5 (i.e., state S0)[6].

Hence the coordinator forms the goal of making his interest known to the sub-contractor and requires a response about the sub-contractors desired terms (if at all) (state S1). Therefore the coordinator makes a *request* to the sub-contractor with respect to his main goal φ and preference φ. There are many possibilities in terms of how the sub-contractor would react to a request. Some of these possibilities are:

1. He may have a clear plan of what tasks he will be carrying out in the corresponding period and sees only one possibility for a cooperation. For instance his only possibility is to transport the orders denoted by ψ.

---

[6] The guide to the representation employed to illustrate the protocols is given in Figure 4.4.

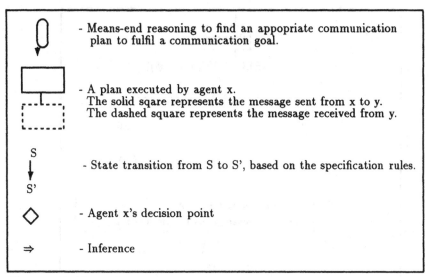

Fig. 4.4. Guide to the representation

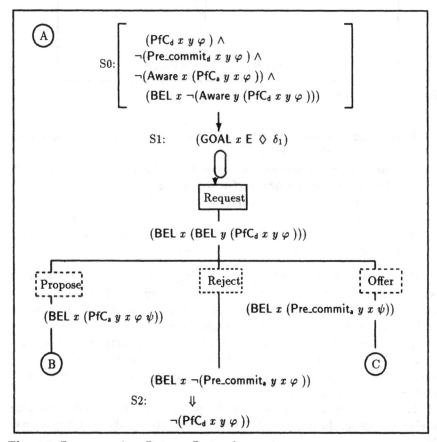

Fig. 4.5. Demonstration: Request Protocol

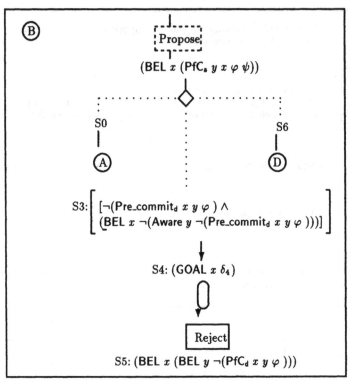

Fig. 4.6. Demonstration: Propose Protocol

In this case, the sub-contractor makes a pre-commitment on his agreed terms ψ and makes an *offer*.

2. The sub-contractor also wishes to negotiate about these terms in which case he will *propose* his own preference (i.e., ψ).

3. the sub-contractor may be completely occupied with other contracts and *reject* the request completely (i.e., reject φ). In this case the coordinator will know that there is no potential for a cooperation and will not follow this possibility any further. (see Figure 4.5, state S2)

One additional option which does not apply to this specific request is when a request made with respect to a goal φ and a preferred term ψ for instance, which denotes part of the orders denoted by φ. In this case, the additional option may be that the sub-contractor is certain that he couldn't meet the coordinators preferred terms (i.e., ψ), and *rejects* the request with respect to these terms. Note that at this stage, it is still possible for the sub-contractor to propose some of his own preferred terms that may be of interest to the coordinator too.

Figure 4.6 demonstrates a possible protocol after the sub-contractor makes a proposal. In this case, the options available to the coordinator may be:

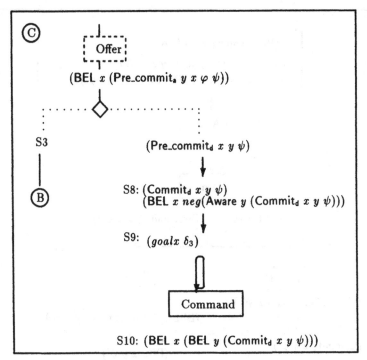

Fig. 4.7. Demonstration: Offer Protocol

1. The coordinator may still see a scope for further negotiation and request new terms (therefore the situation will be similar to state S0 in
   Figure 4.5).
2. The coordinator may be content with the proposal or decide on some
   of his own preferred terms. For instance, that the sub-contractor trans-
   ports orders denoted by ψ'. In this case, the coordinator makes a pre-
   commitment with respect to his agreed terms (state S6, in Figure 4.8)
   and *demands* the sub-contractor to make his final decision.
3. The coordinator may *reject* the sub-contractor's proposal, for instance
   by realising somewhere during the negotiation that some other sub-
   contractor is proposing a better deal, (e.g., states S3, S4 and S5 Figure 4.6).

The possible protocol for after the sub-contractor makes a pre-commitment
and makes an *offer* to the coordinator is demonstrated in Figure 4.7. The negotiation ends either when one of the agents makes a commitment (states
S8-S10 in Figure 4.7 and S12 in Figure 4.8), or one of the agents refuses to
cooperate. In the latter case, the reject plan should reflect the fact that the
agent does not wish to cooperate at all, i.e., reject the potential for a cooperation with respect to any terms regarding the main goal φ. An instance of
such a situation is the states S3-S5 in Figure 4.6, where the coordinator with-

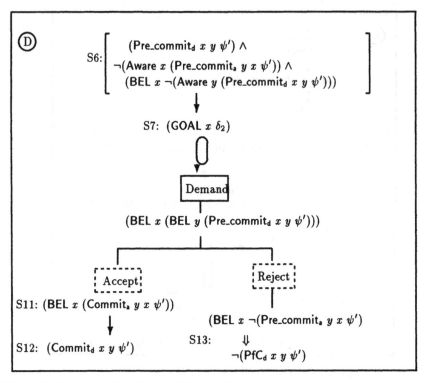

Fig. 4.8. Demonstration: Demand Protocol

draws from anys possibility of contracting out orders to the sub-contractor in question.

It is important to note that the agents could reject some terms but not necessarily reject any other possibility with respect to the main goal φ. For instance, the state S13 in Figure 4.8 refers to the situation where the sub-contractor does not wish to carry out the orders denoted by ψ'. In this situation the negotiation need not terminate if for instance the sub-contractor is still interested in some other terms to cooperate.

The above scenario demonstrated that our theory of agent to agent commitment, not only aids to specify how commitments are formed, but also how agents may reason about each other, and about how to communicate and negotiate on the terms of cooperation.

4.7 Discussion

This chapter provided the specification of the means-end reasoning processes of agents in the context of individual task achievement, task delegation and task adoption. This process was modelled as state transitions involving beliefs, goals and intentions of individual agents and their decisions. The transition from a reasoning state into a future state was specified by a set of rules comparable to the temporal logic specification of the liveness/progress properties of concurrent programs. In particular, these rules specified under what conditions individual and agent-agent commitments are formed, maintained and revised. These conditions were characterised by the convention and the resulting theory of agent-agent commitments described in the previous chapter.

Furthermore, this chapter described how agents reason about communication In this regard, it was argued that at different stages of the reasoning process, agents need to communicate certain facts in order to update their belief about each others attitude towards a possible cooperation and in order to be in a better position to make decisions about whether and how they wish to cooperate. The reasoning behind communication was modelled by specifying the conditions under which certain (sub-) goals that lead to communication are formed. These subgoals are then fed back into the reasoning process to find the appropriate means of fulfilling them. For each subgoal a specific primitive communication plan is designated which become applicable once an agent adopts that goal.

Hence, a rule specifies some conditions that if satisfied lead to adoption of a particular communication goal which in turn lead to the execution of a specific communication plan. An important point to note here is that the conditions specified in each rule in effect give the semantics of a particular speech act. For instance, the conditions specified in Rule 1 in Figure 4.2 give the semantics of the 'request' act in the context of task delegation.

The means-end reasoning process and the execution of the possible communication protocols resulting from this process was demonstrated by means of a transportation and shipping scenario.

Having developed a theory and specified the means-end reasoning processes of agents, the next stage is to describe how this model may be realised in practice. As will be discussed in the next chapter, since an internal theory typically identifies the key data structures (e.g., beliefs, goals, intentions, agent-agent commitments) and the relationships between them, coupling of the theory to an implementable model is more straightforward and consequently the resulting design concepts are justified with the underlying theory.

5. Modelling Interactions in COSY Agent Architecture

5.1 Overview

The purpose of this chapter is to demonstrate how the reasoning about cooperation specified in the previous chapter, may be modelled in a BDI-architecture. The idea is that since the conditions leading to goals to communicate are defined in terms of individual beliefs, goals and intentions, reasoning behind communication can be directly modelled in the general reasoning mechanism of an agent which employs these notions explicitly. For this purpose, the (extended) COSY agent architecture has been chosen. The background to this architecture will be given in Section 5.2, and its top-level components will be described in Section 5.3.

The two components related to the topic of this book are (i) the *Protocol Execution Component*, which administers communication and dialogues, and (ii) the *Reasoning and Deciding Component*, which controls and monitors the (meta-level) reasoning and decisions towards actions and accomplishing tasks. The theory developed in this work has led to the extension of the later component. These components will be described respectively in Section 5.4 and 5.5. Having introduced the architecture, Section 5.6 will describe how in general reasoning and decisions concerning interactions are monitored in the architecture.

The melting-pot of the work presented in this book is Section 5.7 which describes how the reasoning and decisions concerning task delegation and task adoption specified in the last chapter, may be modelled in this architecture. Before concluding this chapter in Section 5.9, Section 5.8 will compare this architecture to some of the other BDI-architectures.

5.2 Background

The COSY (COoperating SYstems) project started out as a research project for establishing methodologies for multi-agent systems, in particular, investigating general control and communication strategies appropriate for a large class of applications. The first results of this project were an agent model and an experimental test-bed for implementing, testing and evaluating various multi-agent scenarios. The test-bed is called DASEDIS [Bur93] which stands for "Development And Simulation Environment for Distributed Intelligent Systems".

In the agent model developed, *behaviours, resources* and *intentions* were identified as the three important elements in the problem-solving of an agent[1] [BS90] [BS92]. An agent's behaviours are classified into *perceptual, cognitive, communicative,* and *effectoric* each of which is simulated by a specific component in the architecture as will be shown later. Intentions are divided into *strategic* intentions and *tactical intentions.* While the strategic intentions model an agent's long-term goals, preferences, roles and responsibilities which in general characterise the agent, tactical intentions are more directly tied to actions, representing an agent's commitment to his chosen plan of actions.

The idea is that based on his strategic intentions and his existing tactical intentions, an agent commits and (tactically) intends to carry out a plan of actions. To execute a behaviour an agent requires resources. Resources are used in a broad sense. For instance, sensing resources (physical sensors, the content of buffers etc.), sending and receiving resources (communication hardware, low-level protocols, bandwidth, message-queues etc.), acting resources (robot arms, time, space, etc.) and cognitive resources (knowledge and belief). An abstract formal description of the agent model is given in [BS92].

The idea of BDI-systems (*beliefs, desires* and *intentions*) that appear to have taken the lead in the theoretical and practical studies of agents was found to share many similarities with this agent model. This triple can be mapped into the concepts behind the COSY model, for instance beliefs are comparable with the cognitive resources, *present-directed* intentions and goals with tactical intentions, and *future-directed* intentions and desires could be modelled as part of strategic intentions[2]. In a sense the triple $<belief, desire, intention>$ could be said to be more specific. The formal theories of BDI-systems inspired the formal theory developed in this work, which in turn led to new modifications and the extension of the COSY agent model.

5.3 COSY Agent Architecture

The design of COSY agent architecture follows a top-down modular method, with modules ACTUATORS, SENSORS, COMMUNICATION, MOTIVATIONS and COGNITION at the top level as depicted in Figure 5.1. The first three modules are domain specific and are modelled by the application designer. The

---

[1] Interestingly, in parallel Shoham also identified very similar notions, namely the triple '*capabilities, beliefs* and *commitments*' as the central elements for agent-oriented programming [Sho93].

[2] Although in the community, there are still debates on the semantics of goals and desires, in lines with the theory, we interpret desires as tasks that an agent in principle is capable of accomplishing, and *goals* as those tasks that an agent has chosen and committed to accomplish.

SENSORS provide up-to-date information about the current states of the environment in which the agent is operating and the events that occur in that environment. The ACTUATORS handle the physical actions of the agent and the COMMUNICATION corresponds to the physical communication specific to the domain. These components will not be further discussed in this thesis. The MOTIVATIONS component models long-term goals of an agent, his roles, preferences and in general the attributes that define his certain characteristics (i.e., strategic intentions). For instance, in presence of a slower vehicle in front, generally a fast driver would usually prefer to over-take than slow down and follow the slower vehicle, but an economic driver would usually try to maintain a steady speed to save petrol.

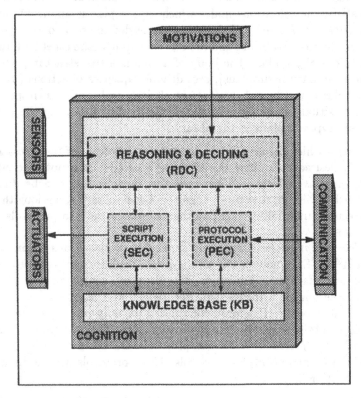

Fig. 5.1. Top Level COSY Agent Architecture

The particular component of interest to this thesis is the COGNITION module which evaluates the current situation and selects, executes and monitors the actions of the agent in that situation. This module is realised as a knowledge-based system. As depicted in Figure 5.1, this component consists of the following sub-components:

- *Knowledge Base* (KB),
- *Script Execution Component* (SEC),
- *Protocol Execution Component* (PEC), and
- *Reasoning and Deciding Component* (RDC).

The beliefs of the agent are modelled by the knowledge base. This includes beliefs about goals, intentions and plans of the agent. Another way of viewing this is that the knowledge base contains all the data structures required by the reasoning processes of the agent. For instance, each agent has a library of pre-compiled plans that resides in the knowledge base. Encoded in these plans are some typical courses of actions to achieve certain desired effects. The application specific problem solving knowledge is encoded into plans.

A plan in general consists of a header and a body. The header includes information such as the name of the plan, the particular desire it is designed to satisfy, the conditions under which such a plan is applicable (called the *invocation conditions*) and the *resources* needed in order to execute the plan. The invocation conditions and the corresponding desire together form the *preconditions* of the plan. The body of a plan is a tree structure, where nodes denote actions (or subplans), arcs denote sequences of actions (or sequences of subplans) and branches represent choices, each choice corresponding to a specific situation the agent may find itself while executing the plan. There are two types of plans in the library:

- *Scripts* which describe some stereotypical sequence of tasks to achieve certain desired ends. The nodes in the structure of scripts are either calls to primitive effectoric behaviours (i.e., actions that can be directly executed by the ACTUATORS), cognitive behaviours (i.e., actions that can be executed internally), calls to other scripts, or calls to protocols described below.
- *Cooperation protocols* represent some stereotypical plans of communication [BHS93]. Each node in the tree is either a call to another protocol or a call to a primitive communication plan. Primitive communication plans denote the sending of a message by the sender and its receipt and processing by the receiver. If a protocol consists of only one node and that node represents a primitive communication plan, then the protocol is called a *primitive protocol*[3]. Primitive protocols are the most primitive building blocks of more complex protocols. These protocols will be discussed later in Section 5.4.

Scripts are monitored and executed by the *Script Execution Component* (SEC) (see Figure 5.1), handing over the execution of primitive behaviours to the ACTUATORS, and protocols to the *Protocol Execution Component* (PEC). PEC in turn, executes and monitors protocols by preparing messages to be sent and administering the messages received within a protocol.

---

[3] Note that a *primitive protocol* has a *primitive communication plan* as the body and certain *preconditions* as a header.

The *Reasoning and Deciding Component* (RDC) resides at the heart of the COGNITION module and is responsible for reasoning about the world and selecting plans appropriate to the given situation and therefore reasoning about how best to achieve goals and fulfill intentions. As part of this process, RDC also makes decisions regarding the branches in the scripts and protocols, that is, while executing a plan, it makes decisions regarding which branch to follow based on the conditions that hold in a given situation. In addition, RDC carries administrative tasks like interrupting plan execution and monitoring decisions. The extension of the architecture is mainly the RDC component whose design concepts rely on the theory developed in this thesis. Since the focus of this thesis is the interactions among agents, in the remainder of this chapter mainly the *Reasoning and Deciding Component* (RDC) and the *Protocol Execution Component* (PEC) will be described.

5.4 Protocols and their Execution

In dealing with communication and dialogues in multi-agent systems there are different levels of abstractions to be considered [BHS93]:

1. message types
2. structure/syntax of messages,
3. procedures for preparing messages to send and for processing received messages,
4. protocols as frameworks for specifying context-dependent patterns of dialogue or the norms of interactions specific to the requirements of the domain.
5. mechanisms to select and keep track of protocols.

To be consistent with the level of abstractions at which all the subcomponents of the COGNITION component is described, messages and message types will be only briefly reviewed, referring the interested readers to [HB93] for more details.

As was discussed in chapter 2 (Section 2.7), according to Austin [Aus62], there is a distinction between the *locutionary, illocutionary* and *perlocutionary* aspects in a speech act. By this, the simple utterance of a sentence (locutionary) is distinguished from its intended effect (illocutionary) and its actual effect (perlocutionary) on the receiver. The locutionary aspect of speech acts falls within the realm of standard communication theory, which in the COSY agent architecture must be modelled in the COMMUNICATION component. In practice, the illocutionary effects are granted by supplementing the sentence to be uttered with a *message type*, that is, the message type determines the sender's intended effect on the receiver. For instance, the message type '*query*', conveys the sender's intended effect that the receiver believes that the sender requires a particular information and that this information must be provided by the receiver. The perlocutionary effects in principle are beyond the control of the speaker/sender of a message. However, in practice certain perlocutionary effects may be enforced, by design. For instance, the receiver must reply to the query as was intended by the sender. Whether the perlocutionary effects must be enforced or not is dependent on the degree of freedom of interaction built into the cognitive capabilities of the agent. This will be discussed further when describing the *intra-protocol decisions* and *active protocol selections* in Section 5.6.

The syntax of messages exchanged by COSY agents is provided in Appendix B. In brief, apart from the *content* of the sentence to be uttered, a message consists of a number of administrative parameters such as addresses of the sender and receiver and the content of the interaction. The *content* consists of a *message type* and an application-specific syntactic construct which denotes the actual fact being communicated[4]. Message types are classified in COSY according to whether a message requires a response or not. This classification is shown in Figure 5.2.

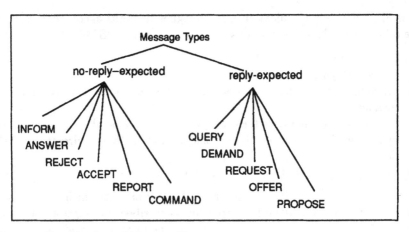

Fig. 5.2. Classification of Message Types

This classification helps keep track of whether a message requires a response. The formal semantics of these message types were given in the previous chapter, by the conditions specified in the rules presented in Figures 4.2 and 4.3 and subsequently by designating to each goal expressed in each rule a specific speech act (denoted as message type, in the design).

The next level concerned with communication, as mentioned above, involves the sending and processing of messages. These are respectively done by a *send-procedure* which prepares a message according to the syntax of messages given in Appendix B and sends the message to the receiver, and a

---

[4] The message types and the syntactic construct respectively correspond to the *illocutionary force* and the *proposition* parts of an illocution (see Section 2.7)

process-procedure which interprets the message received, and routes the interpreted message to RDC. Since most of the meta-level reasoning and decisions must be carried out by RDC, these procedures only have administrative purposes.

Having a brief overview of messages and the procedures for sending messages and processing the received messages, the next level of abstraction deals with *cooperation protocols*.

5.4.1 Cooperation Protocols

The idea behind the cooperation protocols is to provide a framework for designing context-dependent patterns of dialogue specific to the requirements of the domain, to relate messages to their context, enable the communicating agents to keep track of what has been communicated with respect to that context and how the dialogue should proceed.

Once an agent initiates a dialogue within a particular protocol, the receiving agent must use a copy of that protocol in order to respond within the permitted pattern of that protocol. Hence in order for a communication to be successful and the specified dialogue to be carried out, the pair of communicating agents must use a copy of the same protocol (initiated by the sender) throughout their dialogue. The protocols described in this book concern dialogues between two agents. The architecture also allows protocols with broadcasting mechanisms, but their detail is beyond the scope of this book.

The graphical representation of a generic protocol is provided in Figure 5.3. A protocol consists of a header and a body. Apart from the usual parameters in the header part of a plan (such as preconditions), there are additional parameters specific to communication such as addresses of the sender and the receiver of the first message in the protocol, a list of parameters that may be used by the sender of the first message in the protocol and a list of parameters that may be used by the receiver of the first message in that protocol.

The body of a protocol is a tree structure as shown in Figure 5.3, where nodes represent dialogue states, links represent transitions from a dialogue

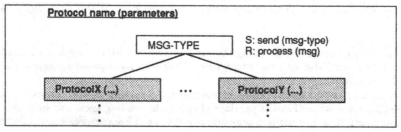

Fig. 5.3. The Generic Protocol

state to another, and branches represent alternative transitions. For consistency and ease of readability, nodes in a protocol body are designated as follows:

- The root node characterises the protocol, and therefore is labeled by the message type which is unique to that protocol. For every protocol there has to be a unique message type to distinguish it from another protocol. The root node represents the state when the first message is sent by the sender and processed after being received by the receiver[5].
- Other nodes are calls to other (sub-) protocols. The text on these nodes are (sub-) protocol names with their required parameters.

In the graphical representation of protocols, the colour of a node represents the active agent (or sender) of the message at that node. A white node indicates that the sender of the first message in the protocol is also the sender at this node. A shaded node indicates that the receiver of the first message in the protocol is the sender at this node.

Figure 5.4 represents some simple protocols. The *Informing* protocol of course is used to provide some information to the receiver. Messages with message types 'INFORM', 'REJECT', 'REPORT' and in general those that require no response are considered as specific type of information and therefore are treated by the *Informing* protocol, with the extra parameter at the header specifying the specific message type. A *Querying* protocol intuitively is used to enquire some information from the receiver. The receiver of the first message processes the query, prepares the answer and invokes the *Informing* protocol (as the sub-protocol of *Querying*) to send the answer. The *Demanding* protocol[6] is used to demand an agent (by default the receiver) to execute a behaviour.

Examples of more complex protocols are given in Figure 5.5. In fact, these protocols (*Requesting* and *Proposing*) are designed to handle likely patterns of dialogue in task delegation and task adoption respectively. The conditions under which these protocols may be called were specified in the previous chapter (see Section 4.4 and 4.5).

Informally, according to this specification, a *Requesting* and a *Proposing* protocol is used to negotiate about a possible cooperation before making a final decision. If the potential for cooperation is first detected by the agent who is attempting to delegate the achievement of one of his goals, then that agent will initiate a *Requesting* protocol. Otherwise, if the first agent who

---

[5] This is represented by denoting the *send-procedure* with its required parameters after the "S:'-label and the *process-procedure* with its required parameters after the "R:"-label.

[6] According to the specification of means-end reasoning in the context of task delegation described in the previous chapter, the sending agent can only execute a demand if he has made a pre-commitment, i.e., (Pre_commit$_d$ x y φ). See also later in Section 5.6.

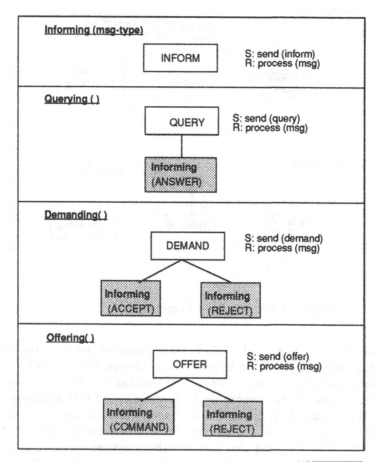

Fig. 5.4. Some Simple Protocols

detects a potential for cooperation is one who is attempting to adopt a task, then that agent will initiate a *Proposing* protocol.

Whoever initiates the communication the other agent must use the same protocol. For instance if an agent initiates a communication by a *Requesting* protocol (i.e., the initiator of the dialogue is attempting to carry out a task delegation), the other agent must use a *Requesting protocol*, process the message received, make a decision and prepare a response. According to the patterns of the dialogue designed into the body of a *Requesting* protocol, this response is restricted to one of (i) rejecting the request, (ii) offering the only possibility the agent agrees to cooperate on, or (iii) proposing one of the agent's own preferred terms of cooperation in the context of the request made. The decision concerning which branch of the protocol to follow is called *intra-*

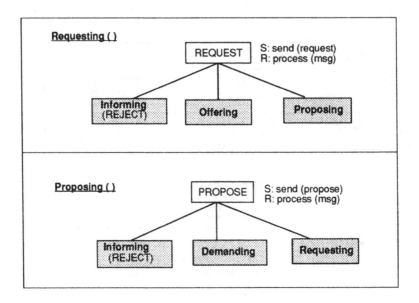

Fig. 5.5. Protocols for Agent to Agent Cooperation

protocol decision. The specification for this reasoning and the intra-protocol decision concerned was given in the previous chapter (section 4.4).

Supposing that the responding agent decided on offering a possibility (i.e., he has made a pre-commitment), he will respond with an Offering protocol. As a result of executing the *Offering protocol* the corresponding *send-procedure* will be called, and the message will be prepared and sent to the requester. After receiving this message, the requester executes his part of the *Offering* (sub-) protocol, interprets the message, makes a decision and responds according to the choices at the branches of the *Offering* protocol, (see Figure 5.4).

The dialogue using complex protocols are limited to the patterns of the body of the protocol, which is compiled at design time. Another alternative would be to enable the communicating parties to build their pattern of dialogue dynamically as they proceed. This means that they could actively choose which messages they wish to send to each other without determining the choices of response expected from the receiver of the message. This is called *active protocol selection.* The protocols chosen in this case are *primitive* protocols. This is comparable to planning using primitive actions versus having pre-compiled plans.

Primitive protocols just like other protocols have a header and a body, but the body consists of only one node (i.e., simply the root node). The agent who initiates a communication chooses (based on some decision criteria) a primitive protocol by which he sends a message to the receiver. The receiver simply processes the message within this protocol and exits it. According to the classification of messages, if the message type of the message sent requires a response then the receiver is obliged to respond, but how he chooses to respond is determined by his own application-specific reasoning and decision mechanism. In the context of negotiation for cooperation, an agent who has received a request may make more queries before making a proposal, an offer or rejecting the request.

Intra-protocol decisions and active protocol selection will be discussed further in Section 5.6.

5.4.2 The Protocol Execution Component

The *Protocol Execution Component* (PEC) makes the protocol components operational, that is, it prepares the required parameters and calls the corresponding *send-* or *process-procedures* denoted at the nodes in the body of the protocol being executed. Furthermore it administers the incoming messages to the particular context that they relate to and the particular dialogue state in that context. This component is activated either when a message is received through COMMUNICATION, or by RDC when a message is to be sent.

Figure 5.6 shows the schematic representation of this component. In the design convention adopted, data stores are designated by round containers and (sub-) modules by rectangles. As mentioned earlier, the *Plans Library* is a library of scripts and protocols residing in the knowledge base.

There are two main modes of operation in PEC: (i) preparing and sending a message, and (ii) dealing with the received messages. When a message is received, the *Message Router* searches the *Suspended Protocols* data structure to see if the message is a response within the framework of a previously initiated protocol. If so, then it resumes the corresponding protocol. This way the message is related to its context and the state of the dialogue in that

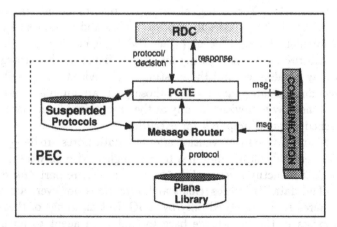

Fig. 5.6. The Protocol Execution Component

context. If however, the message received does not refer to any previously activated protocol, the *Message Router* finds and prepares a protocol for execution based on the message type of the message received. For instance, if the message type of a message is 'QUERY', then the *Message Router* picks the *Querying* protocol, and prepares it for execution by initiating its parameters. In any case, the resumed or the new protocol will be input to the *Protocol Graph Traversal and Execution* (PGTE) module with its operation mode set to 'receive'.

The PGTE may also be activated by RDC. There are two types of output from RDC to PEC: (i) a protocol with its mode of operation set to 'send', and (ii) decision parameters. RDC passes a protocol for execution either as a result of active protocol selection or when initiating a dialogue using a complex protocol. On the other hand, it passes a decision parameter to PEC when a decision concerning an intra-protocol decision is met.

In general, PGTE traverses the protocol to the corresponding dialogue state within the protocol concerned, and calls the corresponding *send-* or *process-procedure* according to the mode of operation specified in the heading of the protocol. Thereafter, it suspends the protocol in the *Suspended Protocols* structure unless the current node is the last node in the protocol, in which case it terminates the execution of that protocol.

5.5 The Reasoning and Deciding Component

The *Reasoning and Deciding Component* (RDC) reasons about which goals to adopt and how to satisfy them according to the given situation. As demonstrated in Figure 5.7, this process logically involves three levels, namely, a *strategic* level (what to do), a *tactical* level (how to do it) and *executional* level (when to do it). The underlying mechanism behind each level is demonstrated in Figure 5.8. The idea is that according to a given situation new goals may be adopted. For each goal the agent reasons about the means of achieving that goal and as a result chooses a plan and commits to the execution of that plan. Finally, the plan that the agent has adopted should be scheduled with respect to his existing intentions. Hence at the strategic level new goals may be adopted and the existing goals revised if required, at the tactical level appropriate plans to meet those goals are intended and the existing intentions may be revised, finally at the executional level, the intended plans are scheduled and prepared for execution.

As before, in the design convention adopted, data stores are designated by round containers and (sub-) modules by rectangles. Also as was mentioned earlier, the data structures *Plans Library* and *Desires* are part of the knowledge base. The data structures *Goals* and *Intentions* however, are local to RDC and therefore are updated only by RDC. But an image of these structures also exists in the knowledge base to enable an agent to have beliefs

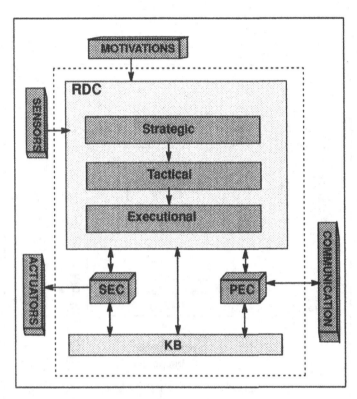

Fig. 5.7. (a) The Reasoning and Deciding Component

about his goals and intentions. As demonstrated in Figure 5.7, the knowledge base is accessible to all the sub-modules of RDC and to SEC and PEC, (which is therefore omitted in Figure 5.8).

The *Desires* structure represents all the possible tasks the agent is designed to achieve. Similarly, the *Plans Library* consists of all the plans (scripts and protocols) that an agent knows about and in principle is capable of carrying out the primitive actions encoded in them. It is assumed that for every desire, an agent has at least one plan of actions.

Like in the theory, goals are distinguished from desires in that they are chosen desires that are consistent and are believed to be in principle achievable, that is, (i) the goal is consistent with agent's beliefs about the current situation, and (ii) the agent has the appropriate plan to achieve the desired ends. Therefore, the *Goals* structure consists of the agent's currently existing goals.

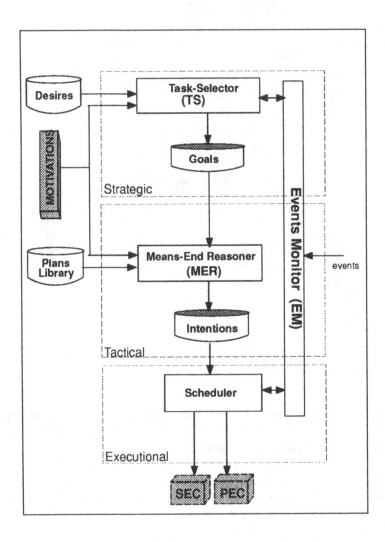

Fig. 5.8. (b) The Reasoning and Deciding Component

The *Intentions* structure is a stack of scripts that the agent has chosen and is committed to execute. The analogy that can be drawn is that while goals are chosen desires of an agent in a given situation that he is committed to achieve, intentions are chosen plans of the agent that he is committed to execute.

Changes in the world are modelled as events. There are three sources of events:

1. SENSORS which capture the important events in the environment that may be of concern to the agent.
2. PEC which filters the messages received from another agent by considering which messages may concern RDC, and convert the corresponding messages into appropriate events.
3. SEC which captures the internal events such as success or failure of execution of plans, or suspension of a script.

The incoming events are routed by the *Events Monitor* (EM) to the other sub-modules of RDC. By default all the events are routed to the *Task Selector*, unless ordered otherwise. This will be discussed later when talking about the executional level of RDC.

Having briefly described the data structures and events, next the sub-modules of RDC will be described.

5.5.1 The Task Selector

The *Task Selector* (TS) observes the incoming events and based on the preferences modelled in the MOTIVATIONS component and the agent's existing goals decides whether new goals must be adopted. If so, then the new goals will be scheduled into the *Goals* data structure. The events input to the task selector may directly relate to the agent's existing goals, new opportunities, or some important changes in the environment that may require rapid response.

This module consists of an application-specific part and an application-independent part. The actual reasoning and decisions regarding whether and with which priority a new goal should be adopted, must be encoded by the application-designers into the application-specific routines. The application-independent part consists of some systems-default procedures which perform administrative tasks, filtering the required information to the application-specific part and monitoring the decisions made to the appropriate destinations. An important fact to be observed when designing the application-specific part is that goals must remain consistent. Therefore, the application-specific part must select among competing goals, determine the existing goals that are in conflict with the new goals, decide if the conflicting goals must be rescheduled or be given up, and schedule the adopted goals with respect to the existing goals. This information (i.e., the new goal priorities, and the existing goals that must be given up) is output to the systems-default procedures which in turn update the *Goals* structure and order the next level in RDC (i.e., the tactical level) to de-schedule the intentions related to the goals that no longer exist. Note that this obeys the *goal-intention* compatibility discussed in chapter 3 (Section 3.3.4, Axiom 2). That is, if an agent intends some option, he must also have that option as a goal.

This architecture also permits the reasoning and decisions concerning task selection to be compiled by the application designer into (meta-level) scripts (see later). In this case, the application-specific part will play no role and the systems-default procedures select the corresponding meta-level goal to select among the competing application-level goals and adds this meta-level goal to the *Goals* structure. Intuitively, in this case, TS would not play a major role in RDC.

5.5.2 The Means-End Reasoner

The main function of the *Means-End Reasoner* (MER) is selecting the appropriate means of achieving the goals in the *Goals* structure. The actual reasoning and decision mechanism for selecting plans must be compiled by the application designer into the body of *meta-level* scripts. Therefore, the problem-solving knowledge concerning the meta-level reasoning and decisions specific to the application (e.g., selecting goals, plans, etc.) is encoded into *Meta-level* scripts.

As a result of this process new intentions may be formed and existing intentions may be revised. Hence the update of the *Intentions* structure is mainly done by MER. This includes rescheduling the intended plans in the *Intentions* structure according to the priority of the goals that they are meant to accomplish (i.e., according to the goal priorities scheduled in the *Goals* structure by the TS module).

The MER module consists of some systems-default procedures which for each goal in the *Goals* structure, search the *Plans Library* and find the plans that if executed successfully would satisfy that goal. This is done by matching the goal to be satisfied and the agents belief about the current situation to the pre-conditions of the plans. If more plans are applicable with respect to a goal, then a meta-level script will be chosen to select one of these plans. Therefore, for each goal initially only one plan is selected and put into the intentions structure. Any other plan related to that goal are later intended as a result of executing the initially selected plan.

As a result of the means-end reasoning process new (sub) goals may be adopted and added into the *Goals* structure and subsequently new plans selected and put into the *Intentions* structure. An important part of the means-end reasoning process in relation to the context of this book is the reasoning about whether and when to cooperate and communicate about a possible cooperation. Goals to communicate are examples of the types of sub-goals that may be formed during this process. The role of MER in this respect will be described in detail in section 5.6 when discussing the reasoning behind communication.

5.5.3 The Scheduler and The Events Monitor

While MER schedules the plans according to the goal priorities in the *Goals* structure, the *Scheduler* actually schedules them for execution by preparing the next script to be executed to the SEC, the next protocol to be executed to PEC, and keeping a record of suspended scripts. This is demonstrated in Figure 5.9. The *Active Scripts* structure contains a top-level script and all the sub-scripts in the body of that script, with a pointer indicating the status of execution of the script and its sub-scripts (i.e, which branches in the script have been followed and which sub-scripts on that branch have been executed).

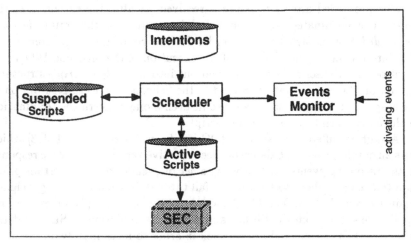

Fig. 5.9. RDC: The Executional Level

The *Intentions* structure may be viewed as a stack, with plan priorities determined by MER. The *Scheduler* removes only one script at a time from the top of this stack and puts it into the *Active Scripts* structure. The next script in the stack is only removed if the *Active Scripts* structure is empty, that is, after the execution of the previously active script was terminated or suspended.

The *Suspended Scripts* structure contains the scripts whose execution were suspended by the SEC because for instance the resources for execution were not available and had to be obtained. Whenever a script is suspended, the scheduler orders the *Events Monitor* (EM) to "keep an eye" on the corresponding event that if occur, the suspended script may be resumed. This is called *active perception*, which means that the perceptual behaviour for detecting the occurrence of an event only becomes active temporarily. When the corresponding event occurs, EM routes the event to the TS module, and to the *Scheduler*. This way, while the scheduler may resume the suspended script, the TS will be informed of what is being executed. For instance suppose the agent is executing a plan to drive from point A to point B. Somewhere while executing the script another goal takes precedence, for example going to the petrol station and filling the car with petrol. The previously executing plan will be temporarily suspended and the new plan (i.e. going to the petrol station etc.) will become active. After the car has been filled with petrol, the suspended plan may be re-activated. This way the TS module knows that the goal to fill the car with petrol has been fulfilled and the goal to reach point B is currently being attempted.

Similarly, if at some stage the current node of the script being executed by SEC denotes a cooperation protocol, then the execution of that protocol is handed over to PEC. At this point, if the execution of the script may only be proceeded after a response is received, or after the execution of the protocol is terminated, then the *Scheduler* would put the script into the *Suspended Scripts* structure and order EM to route the event concerning the (intermediate or final) result of the execution of the protocol. When this event occurs, the script is resumed and put into the *Active Scripts* structure.

Not all the events that are routed to the Scheduler concern resumption of the suspended scripts. For instance some events may concern the termination of the active script or a suspended script.

A slightly different version of RDC has been described in [Had93] which puts an emphasis on the balance between reactive versus deliberative response to the incoming events. In this view, a set of events are given certain priorities that enable them to be directly fall through TS without being weighed against other options. The MER module in this case simply takes the first applicable script from the library and pushes its execution to SEC. But the related details are omitted in this book in order to focus mainly on the parts of the architecture that relate to the reasoning and decisions involved with cooperation.

5.6 Reasoning about Communication

This section describes how in general the reasoning and the decisions concerning communication and negotiation are handled in the COSY agent architecture. The architecture allows two possibilities for reasoning about communication, either (i) the agent actively chooses appropriate primitive protocols based on his goals and preferences and as the situation demands, or (ii) the pattern of communication specific to a particular context of the application domain is compiled into the body of a (complex) protocol, at design time. These respectively relate to the *active protocol selection* and the *intra-protocol decisions* referred to in Section 5.4.

5.6.1 Active Protocol Selection

In this case, subgoals to communicate are formed dynamically and subsequently appropriate primitive protocols are selected by MER. These subgoals are created as a result of executing a script to fulfill a higher-level goal. The need to communicate is passed from SEC which executes the body of the script, to the *Scheduler*. The scheduler suspends the script and passes this information to the *Events Monitor* (EM) which routes it as an event to the TS module. The TS module then selects the related subgoal and schedules it into the *Goals* structure. To fulfill this subgoal, the MER module finds and selects the appropriate primitive protocol and puts it into the *Intentions* structure. The *Scheduler* then passes this primitive protocol to PEC for execution.

As a reminder, the body of a primitive protocol consists of only a root node. Therefore when executing such a protocol, PEC will simply call the corresponding *send-procedure* at that node. On the receiver's side, PEC will execute the corresponding *process-procedure* to interpret the message and pass any decision to be made to RDC. In general at this stage the protocol will be terminated, however, at the sending side if the message-type indicates that a response is required, the execution of this protocol will be considered as successful only after the receiving agent has responded.

Every time a protocol is successfully executed, EM routes the response and some additional information, as an event to the TS module. The TS module removes the related subgoal (i.e., the goal to communicate for which the protocol was selected and executed) from the *Goals* structure, as a result of which MER will remove the protocol from the Intentions structure.

If the response received requires a response to be sent (indicated by the message type of the message received), then the TS module will adopt a goal to prepare this response. The MER in turn finds the appropriate meta-level script in which the corresponding reasoning and decision knowledge is encoded and by which the content of the response will be worked out. Just like the initial script which initiated the need for communication, this meta-level script will be later executed and the subgoal to communicate the response will be formed as a result of executing this script. As before, MER will choose an appropriate primitive protocol to communicate the response, and so forth.

After the communication is complete, (i.e., when no response is to be sent and no response is expected to be received), this information will be given to EM which passes it as an event to the *Scheduler*. The *Scheduler* will take the script which originally initiated the communication, from the *Suspended Scripts* structure and prepares it for resumption according to its priority in the *Intentions* structure.

Active Protocol selection will be demonstrated using an example scenario in Section 5.7.

5.6.2 Intra-Protocol Decisions

As was mentioned earlier, intra-protocol decisions concern the decisions regarding which branch to follow from the current dialogue state (in order to respond) in a complex protocol. This is the same principle as making a decision after receiving a message and before preparing a response, in active protocol selection. The main difference is that (i) the choices for making a decision is limited to the number of the branches descending from the current dialogue state and the nature of nodes at the end of each branch; and (ii) since the protocol names are already designated on the nodes at the end of each branch, there is no need to adopt a sub-goal to communicate and subsequently no need to make means-end reasoning to choose a protocol in order to respond.

Hence, the intra-protocol decisions are made the same way as described above, i.e., by some meta-level scripts which contain the application-specific decision knowledge. But after executing the meta-level script, the resulting decision will be given from SEC to the *Scheduler* which directly passes it over to PEC. The TS and MER are informed only in order to remove the goal and the meta-level script that was selected to make the intra-protocol decision.

Although this alternative is more restrictive in a sense that communication is only limited to the pattern of communication encoded in the body of the protocol, it certainly saves processing time.

In both cases described above, an event concerning for example a request initiated by another agent for a possible cooperation is passed to the TS module, a meta-level goal is adopted by TS and the corresponding meta-level script that makes a decision about this request, is selected by MER. The important fact to note is that if an agent initiates a communication with another agent by choosing a specific (complex) protocol, then the other agent's pattern of response is also limited to that protocol. In this case, RDC will only perform the intra-protocol decisions. Otherwise, that is, if the agent initiating a communication has used a primitive protocol, then the receiving agent is "free" to select how he wishes to respond. In this case RDC will have to do active protocol selection.

This concludes the general mechanisms employed in the COSY agent architecture to handle communication and the reasoning behind communication. Next section will demonstrate how the reasoning and decisions behind communication in the context of agent to agent cooperation specified in the previous chapter, may be modelled in this architecture.

5.7 Modelling Interactions towards Cooperation

Having described how in general the reasoning and decisions involved in interactions are monitored in the COSY agent architecture, this section demonstrates how the theory and the resulting specification for interactions towards agent to agent cooperation may be modelled in this architecture. To aid understanding this section, the example scenario described in the previous chapter (Section 4.6) will be used. The demonstration will be made in the following sequence: first, a summary of the example scenario will be given, then a possible way of modelling the reasoning and decision requirements of the coordinator agent in this scenario will be outlined, and finally, it will be shown how the architecture monitors and administers this model.

Before describing the example scenario, a short resumé of the previous two chapters is provided to refresh their relation to this section. The theory of agent to agent commitments developed in chapter 3 outlined the reasoning for cooperation and communication in terms of individual beliefs, goals and intentions, and the decision constructs 'Willing' and 'Want'. Using these attitudes and the decision constructs, *potential for cooperation*, *pre-commitment*, and *commitments* were defined and the relationships between them specified in a set of axioms. Each of these reasoning constructs were defined once in the context of task delegation and once in the context of task adoption. Based on this theory, chapter 4 specified in this context, the conditions for formations of commitments and the conditions under which certain goals to communicate may be formed.

For the purpose of demonstration, this section concentrates mainly on how the reasoning and decisions concerning task delegation may be modelled in the COSY agent architecture.

The Example Scenario

In summary, the example domain consists of a coordinator who receives orders for transportation and distributes them to the company's transporters (trucks). In the scenario chosen, the coordinator receives some orders that cannot be met by the company's own transporters, as a result of which the coordinator must try to contract out the orders to a private sub-contractor. As in the scenario modelled in Section 4.6, let the coordinator be represented by agent x, the sub-contractor by agent y, and formulae φ, ψ and ψ' represent the following transport orders, where $O_{i,j}$ represents orders to be transported from destination i to destination j.

$$\varphi \quad (transport \quad O_{0,1} \wedge O_{1,2} \wedge O_{2,3} \wedge O_{3,2} \wedge O_{2,0})$$
$$\psi \quad (transport \quad O_{0,1} \wedge O_{2,0})$$
$$\psi' \quad (transport \quad O_{0,1} \wedge O_{1,2} \wedge O_{2,0})$$

Let us start from the point when x has received the orders from the customers and has adopted the goal φ, therefore at this stage the condition (GOAL x $\Diamond \varphi$) holds. We assume that the only means to get φ done is for the coordinator to delegate the achievement of φ to another agent.

5.7.1 Modelling Reasoning and Decisions in Task Delegation

Various states of reasoning and decisions in this scenario were demonstrated in Figures 4.5, 4.6, 4.7 and 4.8, in Section 4.6 in the previous chapter. The problem solving knowledge for evaluation of the conditions characterising these states may be encoded into a number of meta-level scripts as informally described below:

− **Script** q_1: This script attempts to find a possible agent (a transporter or a sub-contractor) using the model of agents represented in the knowledge base. In this example domain, delegating the orders to the company's own transporters has higher priority to contracting out to a sub-contractor. Therefore, contracting out is only considered if the orders cannot be carried out with the companies own transporters. The minimum condition required to be satisfied in order to choose an agent to whom achievement of φ may be delegated, is that a potential for cooperation with that agent exists (i.e., $(\mathsf{PfC_d}\ x\ z\ \varphi))$[7]. Once a possible candidate is found, this plan would cause the goal 'to attempt to delegate φ to the potential candidate' to be formed, (i.e., in this situation $(\mathsf{GOAL}\ x\ \mathsf{E}(\mathsf{Achieves}\ z\ \varphi))$ will hold). Let's φ' be this goal.

    The result of executing this script is a potential cooperating partner which is caused to be entered as an event to the *Task Selector* (TS).
− **Script** q_2: It attempts to delegate φ to a specific agent[8]. This script models the reasoning and decisions behind task delegation, formally specified in the previous chapter (Section 4.3 and 4.4). For ease of reference, the specification of rules to communicate in the context of task delegation are once more included here in Figure 5.10. Encoded in the body of this script are a set of reasoning procedures that evaluate the conditions on the left-hand side of the rules in Figure 5.10 and accordingly cause a goal to communicate to be formed (one of δ_1, δ_2, δ_3, δ_4). As a result of communication belief (and goal) updates about the potential transporter are made. At various stages in this process, the agent also has to make certain decisions that will be discussed later. Through communication and these decisions a pre-commitment and later a commitment may be formed, or lack of a potential for cooperation may be evaluated. Any sub-goals created during the means-end reasoning process to achieve φ will be caused by the execution of this script, and if a commitment is formed, the intention to delegate the task to the other agent is also caused by the execution of this script.

    The final result of execution of this script is any of the following conditions: (i) an agreement is made with the candidate to carry out all the orders denoted by φ, (ii) an agreement is made only on part of the transport

---

[7] See Figure 3.6 in Section 3.4.1, chapter 3, for the definition of potential for cooperation, pre-commitment and commitment in the context of task delegation.

[8] The goal φ and the agent name are a subset of parameters of q_2 that are set when the script is called.

orders denoted by φ, or (iii) no agreement could be made. The final result is registered in the Knowledge Base (KB) and also caused to be input to the TS module as an event.

Rules	Task Delegation
1	$\left[\begin{array}{l} (\text{PfC}_d\ x\ y\ \varphi\ \psi)\ \wedge \\ \neg(\text{Pre\_commit}_d\ x\ y\ (\varphi \vee \psi))\ \wedge \\ \neg(\text{Aware}\ x\ (\text{PfC}_a\ y\ x\ \varphi\ \psi))\ \wedge \\ (\text{BEL}\ x\ \neg(\text{Aware}\ y\ (\text{PfC}_d\ x\ y\ \varphi\ \psi))) \end{array}\right]$ $\rho_1 = (\text{BEL}\ y\ (\text{PfC}_d\ x\ y\ \varphi\ \psi))$ $\gamma_1 = (\text{PfC}_a\ y\ x\ \varphi\ \psi)$
2	$\left[\begin{array}{l} (\text{Pre\_commit}_d\ x\ y\ \psi)\ \wedge \\ \neg(\text{Aware}\ x\ (\text{Pre\_commit}_a\ y\ x\ \psi))\ \wedge \\ (\text{BEL}\ x\ \neg(\text{Aware}\ y\ (\text{Pre\_commit}_d\ x\ y\ \psi))) \end{array}\right]$ $\rho_2 = (\text{BEL}\ y\ (\text{Pre\_commit}_d\ x\ y\ \psi))$ $\gamma_2 = (\text{Pre\_commit}_a\ y\ x\ \psi)$
3	$\left[\begin{array}{l} (\text{Commit}_d\ x\ y\ \varphi)\ \wedge \\ (\text{BEL}\ x\ \neg(\text{Aware}\ y\ (\text{Commit}_d\ x\ y\ \psi))) \end{array}\right]$ $\rho_3 = (\text{BEL}\ y\ (\text{Commit}_d\ x\ y\ \psi))$ $\gamma_3 = \text{true}$
4	$\left[\begin{array}{l} (\text{BEL}\ x\ (\text{PfC}_a\ y\ x\ \varphi\ \psi))\ \wedge \\ \neg(\text{Pre\_commit}_d\ x\ y\ \psi)\ \wedge \\ (\text{BEL}\ x\ \neg(\text{Aware}\ y\ \neg(\text{Pre\_commit}_d\ x\ y\ \psi))) \end{array}\right]$ $\rho_4 = (\text{BEL}\ y\ \neg(\text{Pre\_commit}_d\ x\ y\ \psi))$ $\gamma_4 = \text{true}$

Fig. 5.10. Communciation Rules: Task Delegation

- **Script** q_3: The evaluation of the conditions stated above may require application-specific decisions concerning the scope of compromises that the coordinator is able to make while optimising the fulfillment of his preferences (such as costs, time, etc.). The corresponding decision-making knowledge may be encoded into script q_3.

For simplicity, we assume that script q_3 is a sub-script of script q_2, that is, a call to q_3 is represented at those nodes in which a decision is required so that the aforementioned conditions could be evaluated. Decision-making knowledge may also be partitioned into a number of scripts each of which specialised to make a particular decision, but to keep things simple, this option is not considered here.

Therefore, from the above, script q_1 works out a potential transporter and causes the goal φ' to be formed. This goal denotes the attempt to delegate the achievement of φ to the potential transporter. To achieve φ' script q_2 may be selected. This script evaluates the conditions specified for agent to agent interactions and causes appropriate goals to communicate be adopted as the negotiation proceeds. The decisions concerned in this evaluation are encoded in the body of script q_3 that is called every time a decision is required. After the negotiation with that particular candidate is complete, the result is registered in KB, and caused to be input to TS as an event informing TS of the status of the achievement of goal φ.

To conclude this part, each of the goals to communicate $(\delta_1, \delta_2, \delta_3, \delta_4)$ can be achieved by successful execution of primitive protocols *Requesting, Demanding, Commanding* and *Rejecting* represented in this example by $p_1, p_2, p_3,$ and p_4 respectively[9].

5.7.2 Illustration

The material presented in this section is tightly related to Section 4.6 in the previous chapter. This section will be concerned with two aspects of the scenario described:

1. the reasoning and decisions involved in *active protocol selection*, and
2. how these processes are in general monitored in the COGNITION component of the COSY agent architecture.

The latter aspect is animated in Figures 5.11, 5.12 and 5.13, to illustrate the corresponding control flow in the architecture. The first aspect was already discussed at length in Section 4.6, and the possible state transitions involved were illustrated in Figures 4.5, 4.6, 4.8 and 4.7. To aid the readability of this section, these figures will be side-referenced in the footnotes and not in the main text.

Starting from Figure 5.11 (a), the orders received from the customer are entered as an event to the TS module which does the task selection. The TS module then adopts the goal φ and schedules it into the *Goals* data structure. To achieve this goal, the MER module selects script q_1 and schedules it into the *Intentions* module. When the turn of execution of q_1 comes, the *Scheduler* puts the script into the *Active Scripts* structure to be executed by SEC (the script execution component). Let's assume that as a result of

---

[9] As a reminder, this association was assumed in chapter 4 (Section 4.5).

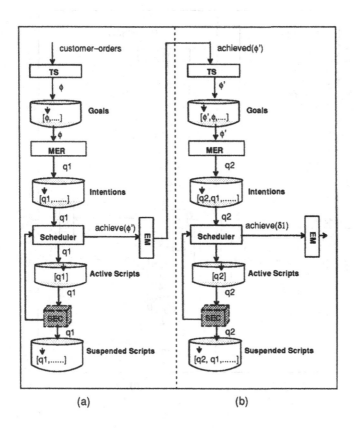

Fig. 5.11. Demonstration: (a) and (b)

executing this script, it is worked out that the company's own transporters are currently unable to meet these orders, and the most likely candidate is the sub-contractor y. After finding this potential cooperator, this script will be suspended and the result (i.e., $achieve(\varphi')$) is passed by the *Scheduler* through the *Events Monitor* (EM) to the TS module. This event will cause TS to adopt the goal φ' to the effect that an attempt to delegate achievement of φ to agent y be made. The TS module then selects and schedules goal φ' into the *Goals* structure (see Figure 5.11 (b)). Therefore, at this stage $(Goal\ x\ \Diamond\ \varphi)$ and $(GOAL\ x\ E(Achieves\ y\ \varphi'))$ hold. Furthermore, since the minimum requirement for considering agent y as a potential cooperating partner is that a potential for cooperation with this agent exists, it is true that $(PfC_d\ x\ y\ \varphi)$ also holds. The MER module then selects and schedules script $q2$ into the *Intentions* structure. Therefore, at this state $(INTEND\ x\ \Diamond\ (Does\ x\ q_1))$ and $(INTEND\ x\ \Diamond\ (Does\ x\ q_2))$ hold.

Let's assume that as a result of executing script q_2, the conditions on the left-hand side of the first rule in Figure 5.10 are satisfied. This means that the

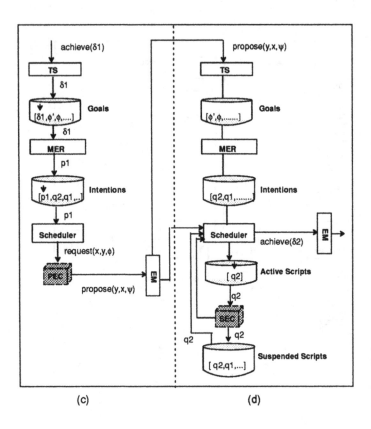

Fig. 5.12. Demonstration: (c) and (d)

goal to make this potential known to agent y and to become aware of whether y agrees with this potential may be adopted. Therefore, the satisfaction of these conditions are passed as an event to TS which in turn adopts the goal δ_1 (see Figure 5.12 (c)).[10] To satisfy this goal, MER selects a *Requesting* protocol and schedules it into the *Intentions* structure. Therefore, at this state (INTEND $x \diamond$ (Does x p_1)) holds. The *Scheduler* then will pass the execution of this protocol to PEC.

Since in our modelling of this scenario, the decision-making knowledge is encoded in script q_3 which is a sub-script of q_2, every time q_2 is suspended for communication, the respond should be returned not only to the TS, but also to the Scheduler in order to resume q_2. Suppose that agent y prefers to carry out the transport orders ψ (which denote part of the orders denoted by φ), but is still prepared to negotiate on the exact terms. In this case, y may respond

---

[10] Referring to Figure 4.5, this corresponds to the transition from state S0 to state S1.

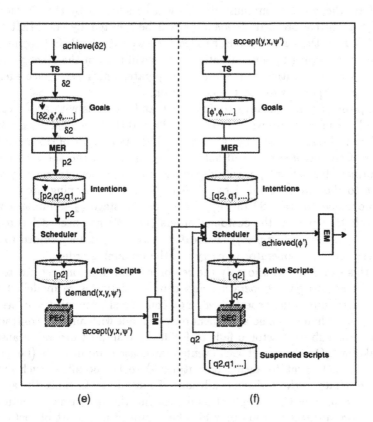

Fig. 5.13. Demonstration: (e) and (f)

by making a proposal (i.e., executing a *Proposing* primitive protocol).[11] The received proposal will be routed by EM, to TS and the *Scheduler* (Figure 5.12 (d)). The TS module then will remove δ_1 from the *Goals* structure, causing MER to remove p_1 from the *Intentions* structure. The *Scheduler* in turn, will resume script q_2 to be executed by SEC. As a reminder, in Section 4.5 it was assumed that any message received from another agent is believed by the receiver. Hence, at this stage, (BEL x (PfC$_a$ y x φ ψ)) holds.

Supposing as a result of executing script q_2, this time the decision returned by execution of the sub-script q_3 is that the only possible compromise x could make is to delegate the achievement of the transport orders ψ' to agent y. This time, the execution of q_2 evaluates and determines that the conditions for adoption of goal δ_2 hold (this is the second rule in Figure 5.10), which means that x has made a pre-commitment to agent y with respect to goal φ and his only preferred terms of cooperation ψ': (Pre_commit$_d$ x y ψ').[12]

---

[11] Therefore, the reasoning process has now proceeded to state S6 in Figure 4.6.
[12] This brings the reasoning process to state S6 in Figure 4.8.

As before, the goal to communicate this will be adopted by the TS module and the primitive protocol *Demanding* will be selected by the MER (i.e., (INTEND $x \diamond (\text{Does } x\ p_2)))$, and handed for execution to PEC (Figure 5.13 (e)). Since according to our convention[13], this will prompt the other agent to either make a commitment or refuse to cooperate, whichever choice agent y makes, this response will end the negotiation.

Supposing agent y makes a commitment, and responds with an *Accepting* protocol[14], this response will be routed to TS and the Scheduler. The Scheduler then will resume script q_2 (Figure 5.13 (f)). As a result of this response, (BEL x (Commit$_a$ y x ψ')) will hold, and according to the specification of commitment formation[15], x will also make a commitment to agent y with respect to the orders denoted by ψ'. Therefore, the reasoning process has now proceeded to state S9 in Figure 4.8. At this stage q_2 terminates with the result that part of the customer orders (i.e., ψ') has been delegated to agent y (i.e., (Commit$_d$ x y ψ')). Thereafter, script q_1 will be resumed to find another potential cooperator to carry out the remaining orders.

In this example scenario only the reasoning and decisions related to the theory of agent-agent cooperation and communication were modelled, but many other important aspects were not considered. Among them are for instance what happens if no agreement may be made with any sub-contractor, or when the sub-contractor y fails to fulfill the transport orders because of a breakdown. Occurrence of such events may cause commitments (i.e. goals, intentions and agent to agent commitments) to be modified. Such events therefore relate to the revision conditions of commitments. Since the agent's reaction to such events is application-dependent, the appropriate reaction as well as commitment revision may also be compiled into a set of meta-level scripts.

This concludes how the reasoning and decisions regarding task delegation may be modelled and how the agent architecture monitors these decisions and enables appropriate interactions to be carried out between the negotiating partners.

5.8 Comparison to Other BDI Architectures

The first known BDI architectures where the mental attitudes of *beliefs, desires* and *intentions* play an explicit and central role in the reasoning mechanisms of an agent, are IRMA [BIP88] and PRS [GL87]. Both of these architectures were inspired by the philosophical work of Bratman [Bra90] discussed in detail in chapter 2.

---

[13] The convention was outlined in Section 3.4.1 in chapter 3.
[14] state S8 in Figure 4.8.
[15] (see Section 4.3.

The design of IRMA (*Intelligent Resource-bounded Machine Architecture*) seems to have pioneered the work on BDI architectures, with the aim of designing an agent with bounded computational resources. The related publications of the authors mainly stress on the role of various deliberation strategies that suggest commitments to already adopted plans are viable strategies for an agent in a changing environment. Apart from Bratman's philosophical background, there is no known logical foundations in support of the theory and specification in terms of beliefs, desires and intentions that is directly linked to IRMA.

Also inspired by Bratman's work, PRS (*Procedural Reasoning System*) is designed for a single 'situated' agent. The loose notion of goals and desires in the original version of PRS were improved upon by the logical system of Rao and Georgeff [RG91c] which also provided the basis for the theory of agent to agent interactions in this book. This logical system was made operational and bound to an interpreter module to construct a BDI architecture in [RG92].

The motivation behind the design of IRMA and PRS was to accommodate the real-time constraints for a single, rational, reasoning agent. These systems are however both concerned with *basic intentional agents* (see chapter 1), but not *social agents*. In terms of the Dennett's *ladder of agent-hood* described in chapter 2, these architectures consider the steps *rationality*, *intentionality* and *stance*, but not the two other steps *reciprocity* and *communication* that make up a *social agent*.

The ideas behind PRS have been adopted and extended in dMARS (*distributed Multi-Agent Reasoning System*) to allow multiply of agents with communication capabilities. But the new system does not as yet offer any general framework for context-specific communication and dialogues comparable to cooperation protocols. In terms of cooperation, some theoretical models have been suggested in [RGS92] and [KLR+94], to enable a team of agents with some pre-compiled social plans to engage in a cooperative activity. These models however have not (as yet) been integrated into dMARS.

Among the BDI-architectures that address some of the requirements of social agents is the functional agent architecture of GRATE* [Jen93]. This architecture at logical level greatly resembles IRMA with additional components to incorporate collaborative problem solving. It utilises the concepts of joint intentions and joint responsibility [Jen92] to establish a collaborative activity and monitor the execution of joint activities, but the relation between the theory and the design is not very obvious.

In addition to the problem-solving components identified in IRMA, such as *Means-End Analyser*, *Compatibility Checker* and *Consistency Checker* which together modify the intentions of the agent, GRATE* includes components to identify potential participants in a team activity and role assignment which, in turn, lead and modify joint intentions. Furthermore, in addition to data structures representing intentions, desires and plans, it includes data structures representing joint intentions, organisational strategies and the agent's belief about other agents' skills. But the design and modelling of the problem-solving components as well as the data structures employed are left to the application designer. Therefore, the architecture does not provide any general mechanism like PRS or COSY where the application-specific problem-solving knowledge mainly only needed to be structured into the body of plans. Also, GRATE* does not provide any mechanisms or methodologies comparable to COSY's cooperation protocols which in our opinion are one of the most important aspects in designing social agents. The functional (or rather logical) architecture of GRATE* is mapped into an implementation architecture which is largely similar to the ARCHON architecture [JW92], [Wit92] but this mapping is loosely defined.

A more detailed analysis and comparison between IRMA, PRS, GRATE* and an earlier version of the COSY agent architecture is given in [HS95].

Among the other related works is AGENT0 of Shoham [Sho93] that was only intended as a prototype. Although AGENT0 does not directly deal with the triple beliefs, desires and intentions, it employs comparable intentional notions (namely, *beliefs, commitments* and *abilities*). The underlying logic[16] appears to be based on [TSSK91]. AGENT0 stresses more on the design of an agent-oriented programming language. In this language an agent is specified by a set of capabilities, and has a set of initial beliefs and commitments. The main problem-solving component which determines the behaviour of an agent is a set of *commitment rules*. As part of their capabilities, agents can send and receive messages. There are only three types of messages that can be exchanged. A 'request' or an 'unrequest' message which lead to modification of commitments, and an 'inform' message which leads to belief update. AGENT0 was later refined and modified in the implementation of another prototype called PLACA (PLAning Communicating Agents) [Tho93], by including operators for planning actions and achieving goals.

As it was noted in [WJ94a], in both AGENT0 and PLACA the relationship between the logic and the interpreted programming language is again only loosely defined. However, one expects that a programming language is more directly coupled to an underlying logic, in a sense that the language can be said to truly *execute* the associated logic. This could also be said with all of the systems described above, including the COSY agent architecture, but neither of these systems are intended as a programming language in the traditional sense. These systems may be considered as some specialised tools for developing agent systems with some general automated features. The underlying logic (if present), is meant to develop theories about certain properties so that the resulting design concepts in terms of the data structures and the relationship between them are in accordance with the theory. But neither of these systems can as yet be theoretically verified and their execution proved

---

[16] The logical framework of this system is a multi-modal logic with direct reference to time. No semantics are however given.

to be correct[17]. Robustness of these systems in many important details must be ensured by the application designer. In this respect, Concurrent METATEM [Fis94]– a framework for programming in temporal logic – is a more promising candidate. But its applicability in practice as an agent-oriented language does not appear to be presently a possibility.

The architectures discussed here are by no means the only ones in the literature, but they are fair representatives. More on agent architectures and languages may be found in [WJ94a].

5.9 Discussion

This chapter described the COSY agent architecture with the modifications and extensions based on the theory of commitments developed in this book. The main modification was made to the COGNITION component by introducing the *Reasoning and Deciding* component (RDC) . The theory identified the intentional attitudes: *beliefs, goals* and *intentions* as the data structures that are revised and modified dynamically; and *plans* and *desires* as the data structures that are assumed to be static. The axioms of the theory, specifying the inter-relationship between these attitudes, provided the concepts behind the design of RDC. RDC is basically a general control mechanism, administering and monitoring the application-specific reasoning and decisions that are encoded in meta-level scripts. These scripts have direct access to the knowledge base where the beliefs, goals and intentions of the agent is represented.

The previous chapter specified the reasoning behind interactions towards cooperation as a state transition process, each state characterised by certain conditions. These conditions were defined in terms of individual beliefs, and the three reasoning constructs *potential for cooperation, pre-commitments* and *commitments*. The process of formation and revision of these constructs is in any case application specific. But since they are defined in terms of individual beliefs, goals and intentions, this chapter demonstrated that the related reasoning and decisions can be encoded into the body of meta-level scripts. Since meta-level scripts have access to the knowledge base, they can represent and modify these constructs locally, and furthermore update the beliefs based on for example, the information exchanged through communication. This way, by encoding the reasoning and decisions behind communication (i.e., active protocol selection and intra-protocol decisions) the reasoning behind interactions can be directly modelled and intergrated into the general reasoning mechanism in RDC.

---

[17] See [RG93] for starting attempts to verification of such systems

6. Summary and Conclusion

6.1 Summary

This book presented a formal yet pragmatic approach to the modelling of agents reasoning about actions and interactions, in particular, demonstrating how communicative actions of agents to engage in a possible cooperation can be derived as part of their general reasoning about actions. The pairwise model of cooperation considered, was an attempt to address some of the problems inherent in more complex cooperative activities of teams of agents.

To model these interactions, an incremental approach was taken: The general process of reasoning about actions was formalised in terms of the interplay of beliefs, desires and intentions. To enable agents to interact effectively, a convention was introduced. Taking the convention as a guideline and using these attitudes as basic reasoning constructs, a theory of commitments was developed defining and specifying the relationships between more complex constructs, namely, *potential for cooperation, pre-commitments,* and commitments. The formal semantics of speech acts employed in the process of negotiating about a possible cooperation was given by specifying the conditions of their execution in terms of the above constructs. These conditions were outlined in a set of temporal state transition rules to model reasoning about communication in the negotiation process.

Since the theory developed is internal and addresses the micro properties of individual agents, it specifies the main data structures and the relationships between them. This provided the basis to the extension and the modification of the cognition module of the COSY agent architecture. The specification rules for reasoning about communication specified the transition from a current state into a future state, each state characterised in terms of these data structures. Therefore, the reasoning and decisions concerning interactions could be modelled and integrated into the general reasoning about actions in the cognition module.

But there are still some open problems and future considerations, some of which will be discussed below.

6.2 Issues for Further study

The semantics of beliefs, goals and intentions in terms of branching possible worlds have enabled us to capture many of their intuitive requirements in the theory, but in practice, it is questionable if these worlds can be modeled and if this modelling will gain us much benefit. In the design of COSY agent architecture, only the interactions of these attitudes have been inspired by the theory, but not their representation.

An adequate way of relating the intentional attitudes to actions and time, is one of the important problems when designing a logical framework for developing agent theories. The intentional attitudes can be effectively modelled in modal logics, using the possible world semantics. On the other hand, action execution can be more appropriately expressed in dynamic logic, where we could explicitly express the pre- and post-conditions of actions as guarded conditions of their execution. For a pragmatic theory of reasoning about actions, we would ideally want to state what a plan or an action can achieve and under what (believed) conditions it may be executed, so that an agent could reason about which plans to choose (i.e., intend) in a given situation and in order to accomplish a given task (or goal). In the framework developed in this book, plans were defined as syntactic constructs, using operators borrowed from dynamic logic. But their pre- and post-conditions are implicit in the semantics of their execution (i.e., the action formulae). Plans and their corresponding pre/postconditions were made explicit by introducing various constructs (such as Achieves and Has_Plan). This model is still unsatisfactory, in terms of the explicit relation that we seek to outline between the intentional attitudes and actions. The problem is that these logical tools provide limited facilities for modelling the intentional modalities and actions, as well as their relationships appropriately.

The model of negotiation considered here was rather simplistic. Negotiation starts with an agent stating (requesting or proposing) a top-level goal that could be achieved in cooperation, and one of its initially preferred terms of cooperation, expressed as a sub-goal of the top-level goal. The agents can therefore only negotiate on which sub-goal they wish to cooperate. Although this is naturally too simplistic and restrictive, it has enabled us to specify examples of under which conditions an agent may communicate and what it may communicate in this process. Nevertheless, other forms of negotiation will have to be modelled in order to examine the strength of this approach.

Different negotiation models result and/or are influenced by the laws, norms, conventions, obligations and in general, social and organisational aspects of the given system. These macro properties also influence other activities in more complex cooperation models involving groups and teams of agents. A perceivable direction to this work is to study if the approach presented could be extended and carried over to the interactions involving team formation, plan generation, role assignment, synchronisation and coordination of activities.

Motivated by developing methods and techniques for agent-oriented systems and their application, this work stressed the fact that an adequate specification of the reasoning processes of agents supported by a formal theory, provides a thorough guideline to the design and implementation of these systems. A related line of research has concentrated on the approaches to the execution of similar specification languages, which may be seen as relating to issues concerning the development of agent-oriented programming languages. These approaches are attractive research topics but their strength in supporting real world applications is currently very limited. Nevertheless, a brief review of these approaches will be given in order to indicate some possible future research directions to the work presented in this book.

6.3 Moving from Specification to Execution

Generally the question to be addressed here is: *given a specification φ, expressed in some logical language L, how do we construct a system S such that* $\{S\} \models \varphi$? [WJ95]. Two general approaches in the literature has been (i) to directly execute φ, or (ii) compile φ into a directly executable form. Both approaches involve generating a model that satisfies the specification. If the agent had complete control over its environment, then model-building reduces to *theorem proving*. But since this is naturally not the case, model-building is an iterative process [WJ95]. Hence, execution and theorem proving are closely related.

Examples of the latter approach are in *synthesis of communicating processes* in concurrent programs [MP84], *synthesis of asynchronous reactive modules* [PR89], and *situated automata paradigm* [RK86]. Generally in these approaches, the specification is expressed in modal logics, the model of which is generated as directed graphs, resembling automata. Therefore execution is a matter of going through the states of the automata. For example, in the *situated automata* paradigm [RK86], roughly, actions of an agent are determined in terms of a set of situation-action rules (encoded in the form of a digital circuit) which are generated by doing constructive theorem proving. This approach looks very attractive but it cannot work for arbitrary (quantified) specifications. Therefore it is questionable how far we can go with this approach.

Fisher and Wooldridge [FW93] describe a programming language called Concurrent METATEM [Fis94], which is based on the direct execution of temporal logic. The general idea here is: on the basis of the past *do* the future. This idea closely relates to the specification rules represented in this book, and it should in principle be possible to execute the specification using this language. But one problem that remains to be addressed in this approach is how informational and motivational attitudes may be integrated into the language. Some work in this direction has been promised.

Both of the above approaches are very attractive but extremely difficult. We still run up against issues concerning the decidability of quantified logic, and the general difficulty of theorem proving. Since both of these ideas in one form or another support execution in terms of *situation-actions*, it seems a reasonable effort to study if the specification rules presented in this book may be executed in either of these forms, and what benefits could be gained as a result.

6.4 Conclusion

This book presented the first attempt to formally represent the process of reasoning about cooperation in a BDI logic and specify how reasoning about communication results from this process. In this attempt a broad range of topics in Artificial Intelligence and Distributed Systems had to be covered and merged together, rendering the task crucially complex and open to rigorous analysis as a necessary precursor.

In developing techniques sufficiently powerful to model a wide spectrum of multi-agent applications, there are many problems and questions to be addressed. On the formal side, the logics employed are very complex, making it extremely difficult to verify and analyse the theories and the techniques developed based upon them. On the practical side, various classes of applications and their typical requirements need to be characterised and appropriate techniques targeted to the problems specific to each class. Yet these techniques should provide an adequate level of abstraction that reduces the complexity of modelling the applications.

All of these are challenging problems. The model of interactions specified in this work represented but an attempt to address some of these problems, suggesting that BDI formalisms provide solid basis for design, specification, and verification of methods and techniques for cooperation and communication in agent systems.

A. Systems of Temporal Logic

This Appendix provides the axiomatisation and Inference rules of various temporal logics. The material provided in here are borrowed from [Woo92]. A good reference is [Gou84] where axiom systems for a number of temporal logics are presented and the soundness of a number of derived axioms is demonstrated through formal proof.

A.1 Propositional Linear Temporal Logic (PLTL)

The list of axioms given here are adapted and extended from [MP81] and [Eme90].

Axioms

Ordinary connectives $\{\wedge, \vee, \neg, \Rightarrow, \Leftrightarrow\}$ obey classical semantics, and thus:

$\vdash \phi$ where ϕ is a propositional tautology.

An obvious and a very useful axiom is:

$\vdash \phi \Leftrightarrow \psi$ where ϕ is defined to be ψ

Axioms dealing with temporal operators:

Equivalence Relations

$\vdash \bigcirc \neg \phi \Leftrightarrow \neg \bigcirc \phi \qquad \vdash \Diamond \Diamond \phi \Leftrightarrow \Diamond \phi$

$\vdash \Box \Box \phi \Leftrightarrow \Box \phi \qquad \vdash \bigcirc \Diamond \phi \Leftrightarrow \Diamond \bigcirc \phi$

$\vdash \bigcirc \Box \phi \Leftrightarrow \Box \bigcirc \phi \qquad \vdash ((\bigcirc \phi)\,\mathcal{U}\,(\bigcirc \psi)) \Leftrightarrow \bigcirc(\phi\,\mathcal{U}\,\psi)$

Forward Implications

$\vdash \phi \Rightarrow \Diamond \phi \qquad \vdash \bigcirc \phi \Rightarrow \Diamond \phi$

$\vdash \Box \phi \Rightarrow \Diamond \phi \qquad \vdash \phi\,\mathcal{U}\,\psi \Rightarrow \Diamond \psi$

$\vdash \Box \phi \Rightarrow \phi \qquad \vdash \Box \phi \Rightarrow \bigcirc \phi$

$\vdash \Box \phi \Rightarrow \bigcirc \Box \phi$

Distributivity Properties

$\vdash \Diamond(\phi \vee \psi) \Leftrightarrow (\Diamond\phi \vee \Diamond\psi)$ $\vdash \Box(\phi \wedge \psi) \Leftrightarrow (\Box\phi \wedge \Box\psi)$

$\vdash ((\varphi \wedge \phi) \, \mathcal{U} \, \psi) \Leftrightarrow ((\varphi \, \mathcal{U} \, \psi) \wedge (\phi \, \mathcal{U} \, \psi))$ $\vdash (\varphi \, \mathcal{U} \, (\phi \vee \psi)) \Leftrightarrow ((\varphi \, \mathcal{U} \, \phi) \vee (\varphi \, \mathcal{U} \, \psi))$

Forward Distribution

$\vdash (\Box\phi \vee \Box\psi) \Rightarrow \Box(\phi \vee \psi)$ $\vdash \Diamond(\phi \wedge \psi) \Rightarrow ((\Diamond\phi) \wedge (\Diamond\psi))$

$\vdash ((\varphi \, \mathcal{U} \, \phi) \vee (\psi \, \mathcal{U} \, \phi)) \Rightarrow ((\varphi \vee \psi) \, \mathcal{U} \, \phi)$ $\vdash (\varphi \, \mathcal{U} \, (\phi \wedge \psi)) \Rightarrow ((\varphi \, \mathcal{U} \, \phi) \wedge (\varphi \, \mathcal{U} \, \psi))$

Monotonic in Arguments [Eme90]

$\vdash \Box(\phi \Rightarrow \psi) \Rightarrow (\Box\phi \Rightarrow \Box\psi)$ $\vdash \Box(\phi \Rightarrow \psi) \Rightarrow (\Diamond\phi \Rightarrow \Diamond\psi)$

$\vdash \Box(\phi \Rightarrow \psi) \Rightarrow (\bigcirc\phi \Rightarrow \bigcirc\psi)$ $\vdash \Box(\phi \Rightarrow \psi) \Rightarrow ((\phi \, \mathcal{U} \, \psi) \Rightarrow (\psi \, \mathcal{U} \, \varphi))$

$\vdash \Box(\phi \Rightarrow \psi) \Rightarrow ((\phi \, \mathcal{U} \, \phi) \Rightarrow (\phi \, \mathcal{U} \, \psi))$

Fixpoint Characteristics [MP81]

$\vdash \Diamond\phi \Leftrightarrow \phi \vee \bigcirc \Diamond \phi$ $\vdash \Box\phi \Leftrightarrow \phi \wedge \bigcirc \Box \phi$

$\vdash \phi \, \mathcal{U} \, \psi \Leftrightarrow \psi \vee (\phi \wedge \bigcirc(\phi \, \mathcal{U} \, \psi))$

Induction Axiom

$\vdash \Box(\phi \Rightarrow \bigcirc\phi) \Rightarrow (\phi \Rightarrow \Box\phi)$

Inference Rules

Propositional connectives have classical semantics, so Modus Ponens (MP) is a rule of inference.

From $\vdash \phi \Rightarrow \psi$ and $\vdash \phi$ infer $\vdash \psi$

The following temporal rules are sound:

From $\vdash \phi$ infer $\bigcirc\phi$
From $\vdash \phi$ infer $\Diamond\phi$
From $\vdash \phi$ infer $\Box\phi$

A.2 First-Order Linear Temporal Logic (FOLTL)

FOLTL contains all the axioms and inference rules of PLTL, and in addition the rules of a first-order logic with equality but no functions. The axiomatisation below is based on [Kro87].

Axioms

Throughout the axiomatisation, the normal form $\phi(x)$ is used to mean that x is *free* in ϕ. Additionally, $\phi[x/y]$ is used to denote the formula obtained from ϕ by systematically replacing every occurrence of y in ϕ by x; i.e., normal substitution.

Universal Instantiation

$$\vdash \forall x . \phi(x) \Rightarrow \phi[t/x]$$

where t is a term that does not occur free in ϕ and x and t are the same sort.

Equality

$$\vdash (\tau = \tau)$$
$$\vdash (\tau 1 = \tau 2) \Rightarrow (\phi \Rightarrow \phi[\tau 2/\tau 1])$$

Barcan Formulae

$$\vdash \forall x . \bigcirc \phi(x) \Leftrightarrow \bigcirc \forall x . \phi(x) \qquad \vdash \exists x . \bigcirc \phi(x) \Leftrightarrow \bigcirc \exists x . \phi(x)$$
$$\vdash \forall x . \Box \phi(x) \Leftrightarrow \Box \forall x . \phi(x) \qquad \vdash \exists x . \Box \phi(x) \Leftrightarrow \Box \exists x . \phi(x)$$
$$\vdash \forall x . \Diamond \phi(x) \Leftrightarrow \Diamond \forall x . \phi(x) \qquad \vdash \exists x . \Diamond \phi(x) \Leftrightarrow \Diamond \exists x . \phi(x)$$

Inference Rule

The only basic inference rule is generalisation.

From $\vdash \phi \Rightarrow \psi$ infer $\vdash \phi \Rightarrow \forall x . \psi$

where there is no free occurrence of x in φ.

A.3 Propositional Branching Temporal Logic (PBTL)

The Axiomatisation of PBTL is adapted from Stirling's axiomatisation of CTL* [Sti88].

Axioms

Ordinary connectives $\{\wedge, \vee, \neg, \Rightarrow, \Leftrightarrow\}$ obey classical semantics, and thus:

$\vdash \phi$ where ϕ is a propositional tautology.

The following deal with temporal/path operators:

$$\vdash \Box(\phi \Rightarrow \psi) \Rightarrow (\Box\phi \Rightarrow \Box\psi) \qquad \vdash \bigcirc\neg\phi \Leftrightarrow \neg\bigcirc\phi$$
$$\vdash \bigcirc(\phi \Rightarrow \psi) \Rightarrow (\bigcirc\phi \Rightarrow \bigcirc\psi) \qquad \vdash \Box\phi \Leftrightarrow \phi \wedge \bigcirc\Box\phi$$
$$\vdash \Box(\phi \Rightarrow \bigcirc\phi) \Rightarrow (\phi \Rightarrow \Box\phi) \qquad \vdash \phi\,\mathcal{U}\,\psi \Rightarrow \Diamond\psi$$
$$\vdash \phi\,\mathcal{U}\,\psi \Rightarrow \psi \vee (\phi \wedge \bigcirc(\phi\,\mathcal{U}\,\psi)) \qquad \vdash \phi \Rightarrow \mathsf{A}\phi \quad \text{if } \phi \text{ is atomic}$$
$$\vdash \mathsf{E}\phi \Rightarrow \phi \quad \text{if } \phi \text{ is atomic} \qquad \vdash \mathsf{A}(\phi \Rightarrow \psi) \Rightarrow (\mathsf{A}\phi \Rightarrow \mathsf{A}\psi)$$
$$\vdash \mathsf{A}\phi \Rightarrow \mathsf{A}\mathsf{A}\phi \qquad \vdash \mathsf{E}\phi \Rightarrow \mathsf{A}\mathsf{E}\phi$$
$$\vdash \mathsf{A}\bigcirc\phi \Rightarrow \bigcirc\mathsf{A}\phi$$

Inference Rules

Since propositional reasoning is sound, modus ponens (MP) is a rule of inference.

From $\vdash \phi \Rightarrow \psi$ and $\vdash \phi$ infer $\vdash \psi$

The following inference rules are from Stirling's axiomatisation of CTL* [Sti88].

From $\vdash \phi$ infer $\vdash \Box\phi$
From $\vdash \phi$ infer $\vdash A\phi$

A.4 First-Order Branching Temporal Logic (FOBTL)

The axioms and inference rules of PBTL are all sound for FOBTL. In addition, FOBTL contains the proof rules and axioms of many sorted first-order logic which largely amounts to ensuring that substitutions are of the correct sort.

B. Syntax of Messages in COSY

A BNF notation of a message is given below:

\<message\>	::	\<header\> \<content\>
\<header\>	::	\<msg-type\> \<msg-id\> \<ref-id\> \<sender\> \<receiver\>
\<msg-type\>	::	"INFORM" | "ANSWER" | "REPORT" | "REJECT" |"QUERY" | "DEMAND" | "COMMAND" | ("PROPOSE" | "REQUEST" | "OFFER" |' "ACCEPT")
\<msg-id\>	::	*ID referring to the particular message*
\<ref-id\>	::	*ID referring to the protocol within which the message is sent/received.*
\<sender\>	::	*ID (name and address) of the sender.*
\<receiver\>	::	*ID (name and address) of the receiver.*
\<content\>	::	\<descriptor\> \<text\> \<agent\>
\<descriptor\>	::	"resource" | "intention" | "behaviour"
\<agent\>	::	\<sender\> | \<receiver\> | \<agent\> | –
\<text\>	::	\<list-of-resources\>| \<intention-name\> | \<list-of-behaviours\>
\<list-of-resources\>	::	[\<list-of-resources\>]* | (\<resource-name\> [. \<resource-value\>])
\<list-of-behaviours\>	::	[\<list-of-behaviours\>]* | \<behaviour-description\>
\<resource-name\>	::	*Name of the resource.*
\<resource-value\>	::	*Value of the named resource.*
\<intention-name\>	::	*Nature/name of the intention.*
\<behaviour-description\>	::	*name or name plus parameters of behaviour.*

Bibliography

[All84] J. F. Allen. Towards a general theory of action and time. *Artificial Intelligence*, 23(2):123–154, 1984.

[AP80] J. F. Allen and R. C. Perrault. Analyzing intention in utterances. *Artificial Intelligence*, 15(3):143–178, 1980.

[App85] D. Applet. *Planning English sentences.* Cambridge University Press, 1985.

[Ash86] N. M. Asher. Belief in discourse representation theory. *Journal of Philosophical Logic*, 15:127–189, 1986.

[Aus62] J. L. Austin. *How to do things with words.* Oxford University Press, 1962.

[BB81] T. Ballmer and W. Brennenstuhl. *Speech Act Classification: A Study in the Lexical Analysis of English Speech Activity Verbs.* Springer, 1981.

[BHS93] B. Burmeister, A. Haddadi, and K. Sundermeyer. Configurable Cooperation Protocols for Multi-Agent Systems. In C. Castelfranchi and J. -P. Müller, editor, *From Reaction to Cognition.* LNAI 957, Springer, 1993.

[BIP88] M. E. Bratman, D. J. Israel, and M. E. Pollack. Plans and Resource-bounded Practical Reasoning. *Computational Intelligence*, 4(4):245–355, 1988.

[Bra84] M. Brand. *Intending and Acting.* MIT Press, 1984.

[Bra87] M. E. Bratman. *Intentions, Plans, and Practical Reasoning.* Harvard University Press, 1987.

[Bra90] M. E. Bratman. What is Intention? In P. R. Cohen, J. Morgan, and M. E. Pollack, editors, *Intentions in Communication*, pages 15–31. MIT Press, 1990.

[BS90] B. Burmeister and K. Sundermeyer. COSY: Towards a Methodology of Multi-Agent Systems. In *Draft Proc. CKBS-90*, 1990.

[BS92] B. Burmeister and K. Sundermeyer. Cooperative Problem-Solving Guided by Intentions and Perception. In E. Werner and Y. Demazeau, editors, *Decentralized A. I. 3*, pages 77–92. Elsvier Science Publishers, 1992.

[Bur93] B. Burmeister. DASEDIS - Eine Entwicklungsumgebung zum Agenten-Orientierten Programieren. In J. Müler, editor, *Verteilter Künsliche Intelligenz, Methoden und Anwendungen*, pages 257–265. Wissenschaftsverlag, 1993.

[CC93] R. Conte and C. Castelfranchi. Norms as mental objects. From normative beliefs to normative goals. In *Reasoning about Mental States: Formal Theories and Applications, spring symposium.* AAAI Press, 1993.

[CD90] J. A. Campbell and P. D'Inverno. Knowledge Interchange Protocols. In Y. Demazeau and J. P. Müller, editor, *Decentralized A.I.* Elsevier/North-Holland, 1990.

[Che80] B. Chellas. *Modal Logic: An Introduction.* Cambridge University Press, 1980.

[Chu81] Paul M. Churchland. eliminative materialism and the propositional attitudes. *Journal of Philosophy*, 78:67–90, 1981.

[Chu88] Paul M. Churchland. On the Ontological Status of Intentional States: Nailing Folk Psychology to Its Perch. *Behavioural and Brain Sciences*, 11(3):507–508, 1988.

[CL86] P. R. Cohen and H. J. Levesque. Persistence, intention and commitment. In M. P. Georgeff and A. L. Lansky, editors, *Proc. Timberline Workshop on Reasoning about plans and actions*, pages 297–338, 1986.

[CL88] P. R. Cohen and H. J. Levesque. Rational Interaction as the Basis for Communication. Technical Report 433, SRI International, 1988.

[CL90] P. R. Cohen and H. J. Levesque. Intention Is Choice with Commitment. *Artificial Intelligence*, 42:213–261, 1990.

[CL91] P. R. Cohen and H. J. Levesque. TEAMWORK. Technical report, SRI International, Technote 504, 1991.

[Con89] R. Conte. Institutions and Intelligent Systems. In M. Jackson, P. Keys, and s. Cooper, editors, *Operational Research and the Social Sciences*, 1989.

[CP79] P. R. Cohen and C. R. Perrault. Elements of a Plan-Based Theory of Speech Acts. *Cognitive Science*, 3(3):177–212, 1979.

[CST92] Patricia S. Churchland, S. Sejnowski, and J. Terrence. *The Computational Brain*. Cambridge MA, London: MIT Press, 1992.

[CW92] Man Kit Chang and C. C. Woo. SANP: A Communication Level Protocol for Negotiations. In E. Werner and Y. Demazeau, editors, *Decentralized A.I.3*. North-Holland, 1992.

[Den81] D. C. Dennett. *Brainstorms*. Harvester Press, 1981.

[Den91] D. C. Dennett. *Consciousness Explained*. Little, Brown & Co., 1991.

[dGCM92] P. de Greef, K. Clark, and F. McCabe. Toward a Specification Language for Cooperation Methods. In *GWAI-92 Workshop Supporting Collaborative Work Between Human Experts and Intelligent Cooperative Information Systems*, 1992.

[DM90] E. H. Durfee and T. A. Montgomery. A Hierarchical Protocol for Coordinating Multiagent Behavior. In *Proc. AAAI-90*, 1990.

[DS83] R. Davis and R. G. Smith. Negotiation as a Metaphor for Distributed Problem Solving. *Artificial Intelligence*, 20:63–109, 1983.

[Ebe74] R. A. Eberle. A Logic of Believing, Knowing and Inferring. *Synthese 26*, pages 356–382, 1974.

[Eme90] E. A. Emerson. Temporal and Modal Logic. In J. van Leeuwen, editor, *Handbook of Theoretical Computer Science*, volume B. Elsvier Science Publishers B. V., 1990.

[FH85] R. Fagin and J. Y. Halpern. Belief, Awareness, and Limited Reasoning. In *Proc. of IJCAI-85*. Morgen Kaufmann, 1985.

[Fis94] M. Fisher. A survey of Concurrent METATEM - the language and its applications. In D. Gabbay and H.-J. Ohlbach, editors, *Proc. of the First Int. Conf. on Temporal Logic (ICTL-94)*. Springer-Verlag, 1994.

[Foo89] A. S. Rao N. Y. Foo. Minimal Change and Maximal Coherence: A Basis for Belief Revision and Reasoning about Actions. In *Proc. IJCAI-89*, pages 966–970, 1989.

[FW93] M. Fisher and M. Wooldridge. Executable temporal logic for distributed A. I. In *Proc. of the 12th International Workshop on Distributed Artificial Intelligence (IWDAI-93)*, pages 131–142, 1993.

[GD93] P. J. Gmytrasiewicz and E. H. Durfee. Reasoning about Other Agents: Philosophy, Theory, and Implementation. In *Proc. of the 12th International Workshop on Distributed AI*, 1993.

[GI88] M. P. Georgeff and F. F. Ingrand. Research on procedural reasoning systems. Technical report, AI Center, SRI International, Menlo park, California, 1988. Final Report, phase 1.

[GL87] M. P. Georgeff and A. L. Lansky. Reactive Reasoning and Planning. In *Proc. AAAI-87*, pages 677–682, 1987.

[GL93] R. P. Goldman and R. R. Lang. Intentions in Time. Technical report, TUTR 93-101, Center for Autonomous Complex Systems, Tulane University, 1993.

[Gou84] G. D. Gough. Decision Procedures for Temporal Logic. Master's thesis, University of Manchester, UK, 1984.

[GS90] B. Grosz and C. Sidner. Plans for Discourse. In P. R. Cohen, J. Morgan, and M. E. Pollack, editors, *Intentions in Communication*. MIT Press, 1990.

[Had93] A. Haddadi. A Hybrid Architecture for Multi-Agent Systems. In *Proc. of the Workship on Cooperative Knowledge-Based Systems (CKBS-93)*, pages 13–25, Keele, UK, 1993.

[Hal86] J. Y. Halpern. Reasoning About Knowledge: An Overview (invited talk). In J. Y. Halpern, editor, *Proc. Theoretical Aspects of Reasoning About Knowledge*, pages 1–18, 1986.

[Har79] D. Harel. *First-Order Dynamic Logic*. Springer-Verlag, 1979.

[HB93] A. Haddadi and B. Burmeister. Cooperation Protocols. Technical report, COSY internal report, Damiler-Benz Reseach Institute, Berlin, 1993.

[HB94] A. Haddadi and S. Bussmann. Scheduling Meetings using Negotiation. In *Coordination Design and Planning Workshop, CAIA-94*, San Antonio, Texas, 1994.

[Hin62] J. Hintikka. *Knowledge and Belief*. Cornell University Press, 1962.

[Hin72] J. Hintikka. Semantics for propositional attitudes. In L. Linsky, editor, *Reference and Modality*. Oxford University Press, 1972.

[HM85] J. Y. Halpern and Y. Moses. Knowledge and Common Knowledge in a Distributed Environment. In *Proc. of the Third ACM Symposium on the Principles of Distributed Computing*, pages 50–61, 1985.

[HM92] J. Y. Halpern and Y. Moses. A Guide to Completeness and Complexity for Modal Logics of Knowledge and Belief. *Artificial Intelligence*, 54(3):319–379, 1992.

[HS93] A. Haddadi and K. Sundermeyer. Acquaintance Relations in Autonomous Agent Societies. In *ISADS-93*, Kawasaki, Japan, 1993.

[HS95] A. Haddadi and K. Sundermeyer. Belief, Desire, Intention Agent Architectures. In N. Jennings and G. O'Hare, editors, *Foundations of Distributed Artificial Intelligence*. Wiley Inter-Science, 1995.

[Jen92] N. R. Jennings. *Joint Intentions as a Model of Multi-Agent Cooperation*. PhD thesis, Queen Mary and Wesfield Colledge, Department of Electrical Engineering, University of London, technical report 92/18, 1992.

[Jen93] N. R. Jennings. Specification and Implementation of Belief-Desire-joint-Intention Architecture for Collaborative Problem Solving. In *International Journal of Intelligent and Cooperative Information Systems*, 1993.

[Jon90] C. Jones. *Systematic Software Development Using VDM*. Prentice Hall, 1990.

[JW92] N. R. Jennings and T. Wittig. ARCHON: Theory and Practice. In *Intelligent Systems Engineering*, volume 1:2, pages 102–114, 1992.

[Kis92] G. Kiss. Variable Coupling of Agents to their Environment: Combining Situated and Symbolic Automata. In Y. Demazeau and J. P. Müller, editor, *Decentralized A.I.3*, pages 231–248. North-Holland, 1992.

[KLR+94] D. Kinny, M. Ljungberg, A. Rao, E. Sonenberg, G. Tidhar, and E. Werner. Planned Team Activity. In C. Castelfranchi and E. Werner, editors, *Artificial Social Systems, Lecture Notes in Artificial Intelligence, 830*, pages 226–256. Springer-Verlag, 1994.

[Kon86a] K. Konolige. *A Deduction Model of Belief*. Pitman/Morgan Kaufmann, 1986.

[Kon86b] K. Konolige. What Awareness Isn't: A Sentential View of Implicit and Explicit Belief. In J. Y. Halpern, editor, *Proc. Theoretical Aspects of Reasoning About Knowledge*, pages 241–250, 1986.

[KP93] K. Konolige and M. E. Pollack. A representationalist theory of intention. In *Proc. of 13th International Joint Conference on Artificial Intelligence (IJCAI-93)*, 1993.

[Kri63] S. A. Kripke. Semantical analysis of modal logic. *Zeitschrift fuer Mathematische Logik und Grundlagen der Mathematik*, 9:67–96, 1963.

[Kro87] F. Kroeger. Temporal Logic of Programs. In *EATCSs Monographs on Theoretical Computer Science Vol 8*. Springer-Verlag, 1987.

[KvM91] T. Kreifelts and F. von Martial. A Negotiation Framework for Autonomous Agents. In Y. Demazeau and J. P. Müller, editor, *Decentralized A.I.2*. Elsevier/North-Holland, 1991.

[Lak86] G. Lakemeyer. Steps Towards a First-order Logic of Explicit and Implicit Belief. In J. Y. Halpern, editor, *Proc. of the 1986 Conference on Theoretical Aspects of Reasoning About Knowledge*. Morgan Kaufmann, 1986.

[LCN90] H. J. Levesque, P. R. Cohen, and J. H. T. Nunes. On Acting Together. In *Proc. AAAI-90*, pages 94–99, 1990.

[Lev81] S. C. Levinson. The Essential Inadequacies of Speech Act Models of Dialogue. In H. Parrett, editor, *Possibilities and Limitations of Pragmatics*, 1981.

[Lev84] H. J. Levesque. A logic of Implicit and Explicit Belief. In *Proc. AAAI-84*. Morgan Kaufmann, 1984.

[McA88] G. L. McArthur. Reasoning about knowledge and belief: a survey. *Computational Intelligence*, 4:223–243, 1988.

[Moo85] R. C. Moore. A Formal Theory of Knowledge and Action. In J. R. Hobbs and R. C. Moore, editors, *Formal Theories of the Commonsense World*. Ablex Publishing Corporation, 1985.

[Mor86] L. Morgenstern. A First Order Theory of Planning, Knowledge, and Action. In J. Y. Halpern, editor, *Proc. of the 1986 Conference on Theoretical Aspects of Reasoning About Knowledge*. Morgan Kaufmann, 1986.

[MP81] Z. Manna and A. Pnueli. Verification of Concurrent Programs: The Temporal Framework. In R. S. Boyer and J. S. Moore, editors, *The Correctness Problem in Computer Science*. Academic Press, London, 1981.

[MP84] Z. Manna and A. Pnueli. Synthesis of communicating processes from temporal logic specifications. *ACM Transactions on Programming Languages and Systems*, 6(1):68–93, 1984.

[Nar91] Narayanan. *On Being a Machine*. Ellis Horwood, 1991.

[PC95] M. Pickering and N. Chater. Why Cognitive Science Is Not Formalized Folk Psychology. *Minds and Machines*, 5(3):309–337, 1995.

[Pnu77] A. Pnueli. The Temporal Logic of programs. In *Proc. 18th Ann. IEEE symp. on Foundations of Computer Science*, pages 46–57, 1977.

[Pol90] M. E. Pollack. Plans as Complex Mental Attitudes. In P. R. Cohen, J. Morgan, and M. E. Pollack, editors, *Intentions in Communication*. MIT Press, 1990.

[PR89] A. Pnueli and R. Rosner. On the synthesis of an asynchrinous reactive module. In *Proceedings of the 6th International Colloquium on Automata, Langugages, and Programs*, 1989.

[PS85] P. F. Patel-Schneider. A Decidable First-order Logic for Knowledge representation. In *Proc. of IJCAI-85*, pages 455–458. Morgen Kaufmann, 1985.

[Rei89] H. Reichgelt. Logics for Reasoning About Knowledge and Belief. *Knowledge Engineering Review*, 4(2), 1989.

[RG91a] A. S. Rao and M. P. Georgeff. Asymmetry Thesis and Side-Effect Problems in Linear-Time and Branching-Time Intention Logics. In *Proc. IJCAI-91*, pages 498–504, 1991.

[RG91b] A. S. Rao and M. P. Georgeff. Deliberation and its Role in the Formation of Intentions. In *Proc. 7th Conf. on Uncertainty in Artificial Intelligence*, pages 300–307, 1991.

[RG91c] A. S. Rao and M. P. Georgeff. Modeling Rational Agents within a BDI Architecture. In J. Allen, R. Fikes, and E. Sandwall, editors, *Proc. of the Int. Conf. on Principles of Knowledge Representation and Reasoning, (KR-91)*, pages 473–484, San Mateo, CA, 1991. Morgan Kaufmann.

[RG92] A. S. Rao and M. P. Georgeff. An Abstract Architecture for Rational Agents. In B. Nebel, C. Rich, and W. Swartout, editors, *Proc. of the Int. Conf. on Principles of Knowledge Representation and Reasoning (KR-92)*, pages 439–449, San Mateo, CA, 1992. Morgan Kaufmann.

[RG93] A. S. Rao and M. P. Georgeff. A Model-Theoretic Approach to the Verification of Situated Reasoning Systems. In *Proc. IJCAI-93*, pages 318–324, 1993.

[RGS92] A. S. Rao, M. P. Georgeff, and E. A. Sonnenberg. Social Plans: A Preliminary Report. In E. Werner and Y. Demazeau, editors, *Decentralized A. I. 3*. Elsevier Science Publishers, 1992.

[RK86] S. Rosenschein and L. Kaelbling. The synthesis of digital machines with provable epistemic properties. In J. Y. Halpern, editor, *Proc. Theoretical Aspects of Reasoning About Knowledge*, pages 83–98, 1986.

[SA92] M. P. Singh and N. M. Asher. A logic of intentions and beliefs. *Journal of Philosophical Logic*, 1992.

[Sad92] M. D. Sadek. A Study in the Logic of Intention. In *Proc. Conf. Knowledge Representation and Reasoning, (KR-92)*, 1992.

[SC94] Y. Shoham and S. B. Cousins. Logics of Mental Attitudes in AI. In G. Lakemeyer and B. Nebel, editors, *Foundations of Knowledge Representation and Reasoning, Lecture Notes in AI*. Springer Verlag, 1994.

[Sea69] J. R. Searle. *Speech Acts*. Cambridge University Press, 1969.

[Sea83] J. R. Searle. *Intentionality: An Essay in the Philosophy of Mind*. Cambridge University Press, 1983.

[Sea90] J. R. Searle. Collective Intentions and Actions. In P. R. Cohen, J. Morgan, and M. E. Pollack, editors, *Intentions in Communication*, pages 401–415. MIT Press, 1990.

[See89] Nigel Seel. Formalising first-order Intentional Systems Theory. Technical report, STC Technology LTD, 1989.

[Sho93] Y. Shoham. Agent-oriented programming. *Artificial Intelligence*, 60(1):51–92, 1993.

[Sho94] Y. Shoham. Micro and Macro Theories of Artificial Agents. In C. Castelfranchi and E. Werner, editors, *Artificial Social Systems, Lecture Notes in Artificial Intelligence, 830*. Springer-Verlag, 1994.

[Sin91a] M. P. Singh. Group Ability and Structure. In Y. Demazeau and J. P. Müller, editor, *Decentralized A. I.2*. Elsevier/North-Holland, 1991.

[Sin91b] M. P. Singh. Group Intentions. In *Proceedings of the 10th International Workshop on Distributed Artificial Intelligence*. MCC Technical Report Number ACT-AI-355-90, 1991.

[Sin92] M. P. Singh. A Critical Examination of the Cohen-Levesque Theory of Intentions. In *Proc. European Conference in Artificial Intelligence, (ECAI-92)*, 1992.

[Sin95] M. P. Singh. *Multiagent Systems: A Theoretical Framework for Intentions, Know-How, and Communications*. Springer Verlag, Lecture Notes in Computer Science, volume 799, 1995.

[Smi80] R. G. Smith. The Contract Net Protocol: High-Level Communication and Control in a Distributed Problem Solver. *IEEE Transactions on Computers C-29*, 1980.

[Smi91] T. Smithers. Taking Eliminative Materialism Seriously: A Methodology for Autonomous Systems Research. In F. J. Varela and P. Bourgine, editors, *Towards a Practice of Autonomous Systems, Proceedings of the 1st European Conference on Artificial Life*, 1991.

[Sti88] C. Stirling. Completeness results for full branching time logic. *REX School -Workshop on linear Time, Branching Time,, and Partial Order in Logics and Modells for Concurrency*, 1988.

[Syc88] K. Sycara. Resolving Goal-Conflicts via Negotiation. In *Proc. AAAI-88*, 1988.

[Tho93] S. R. Thomas. *PLACA, an Agent Oriented Programming Language*. PhD thesis, Computer Science Department, Stanford University, Stanford, CA, 1993. (Available as technical report STAN-CS-93-1487).

[TM88] R. Tuomela and K. Miller. We-intentions. In *Philosophical Studies 53*, pages 367–389, 1988.

[TSSK91] S. R. Thomas, Y. Shoham, A. Schwartz, and S. Kraus. Preliminary thoughts on an agent description language. *International Journal of Intelligent Systems*, 6:497–508, 1991.

[Tuo94] R. Tuomela. Philosophy and Distributed Artificial Intelligence: The Case of Joint Intention. In N. Jennings and G. O'Hare, editors, *Foundations of Distributed Artificial Intelligence*. Wiley Inter-Sience, 1994.

[vV93] Hans van Vilet. *Software Engineering, Principles and Practice*. John Wiley & Sons, 1993.

[WF86] T. Winograd and F. Flores. *Understanding Computers and Cognition*. Addison-Wesley, 1986.

[Wit92] T. Wittig. *ARCHON - an architecture for multi-agent systems*. Ellis Horwood, 1992.

[WJ94a] M. J. Wooldridge and N. R. Jennings. Agent Theories, Architectures, and Languages: A Survey. In *Pre-proceedings of the 1994 Workshop on Agent Theories, Architectures, and Languages, ECAI-94*, pages 1–32, 1994.

[WJ94b] M. J. Wooldridge and N. R. Jennings. Formalising the Cooperative Problem Solving Process. In *Proc. od the European Workshop on modelling Autonomous Agents in Mulit-Agent World (MAAMAW-94)*, 6th, pages 403–417, Odense, Denmark, 1994.

[WJ95] M. J. Wooldridge and N. R. Jennings. Intelligent Agents: Theory and Practice. *Knowledge Engineering Review*, 10(2), 1995.

[Woo92] M. J. Wooldridge. *The logical Modelling of Computational Multi-agent Systems*. PhD thesis, Department of Computation, UMIST, Manchester, 1992.

[Woo94] M. J. Wooldridge. Coherent Social Action – A Formal Analysis. In *11th European conference on Artificial Intelligence, (ECAI-94)*, 1994.

Lecture Notes in Artificial Intelligence (LNAI)

Vol. 898: P. Steffens (Ed.), Machine Translation and the Lexicon. Proceedings, 1993. X, 251 pages. 1995.

Vol. 904: P. Vitányi (Ed.), Computational Learning Theory. EuroCOLT'95. Proceedings, 1995. XVII, 415 pages. 1995.

Vol. 912: N. Lavrăç S. Wrobel (Eds.), Machine Learning: ECML – 95. Proceedings, 1995. XI, 370 pages. 1995.

Vol. 918: P. Baumgartner, R. Hähnle, J. Posegga (Eds.), Theorem Proving with Analytic Tableaux and Related Methods. Proceedings, 1995. X, 352 pages. 1995.

Vol. 927: J. Dix, L. Moniz Pereira, T.C. Przymusinski (Eds.), Non-Monotonic Extensions of Logic Programming. Proceedings, 1994. IX, 229 pages. 1995.

Vol. 928: V.W. Marek, A. Nerode, M. Truszczynski (Eds.), Logic Programming and Nonmonotonic Reasoning. Proceedings, 1995. VIII, 417 pages. 1995.

Vol. 929: F. Morán, A. Moreno, J.J. Merelo, P.Chacón (Eds.), Advances in Artificial Life. Proceedings, 1995. XIII, 960 pages. 1995.

Vol. 934: P. Barahona, M. Stefanelli, J. Wyatt (Eds.), Artificial Intelligence in Medicine. Proceedings, 1995. XI, 449 pages. 1995.

Vol. 941: M. Cadoli, Tractable Reasoning in Artificial Intelligence. XVII, 247 pages. 1995.

Vol. 946: C. Froidevaux, J. Kohlas (Eds.), Symbolic Quantitative and Approaches to Reasoning under Uncertainty. Proceedings, 1995. X, 430 pages. 1995.

Vol. 954: G. Ellis, R. Levinson, W. Rich. J.F. Sowa (Eds.), Conceptual Structures: Applications, Implementation and Theory. Proceedings, 1995. IX, 353 pages. 1995.

Vol. 956: X. Yao (Ed.), Progress in Evolutionary Computation. Proceedings, 1993, 1994. VIII, 314 pages. 1995.

Vol. 957: C. Castelfranchi, J.-P. Müller (Eds.), From Reaction to Cognition. Proceedings, 1993. VI, 252 pages. 1995.

Vol. 961: K.P. Jantke. S. Lange (Eds.), Algorithmic Learning for Knowledge-Based Systems. X, 511 pages. 1995.

Vol. 981: I. Wachsmuth, C.-R. Rollinger, W. Brauer (Eds.), KI-95: Advances in Artificial Intelligence. Proceedings, 1995. XII, 269 pages. 1995.

Vol. 984: J.-M. Haton, M. Keane, M. Manago (Eds.), Advances in Case-Based Reasoning. Proceedings, 1994. VIII, 307 pages. 1995.

Vol. 990: C. Pinto-Ferreira, N.J. Mamede (Eds.), Progress in Artificial Intelligence. Proceedings, 1995. XIV, 487 pages. 1995.

Vol. 991: J. Wainer, A. Carvalho (Eds.), Advances in Artificial Intelligence. Proceedings, 1995. XII, 342 pages. 1995.

Vol. 992: M. Gori, G. Soda (Eds.), Topics in Artificial Intelligence. Proceedings, 1995. XII, 451 pages. 1995.

Vol. 997: K. P. Jantke, T. Shinohara, T. Zeugmann (Eds.), Algorithmic Learning Theory. Proceedings, 1995. XV, 319 pages. 1995.

Vol. 1003: P. Pandurang Nayak, Automated Modeling of Physical Systems. XXI, 232 pages. 1995.

Vol. 1010: M. Veloso, A. Aamodt (Eds.), Case-Based Reasoning Research and Development. Proceedings, 1995. X, 576 pages. 1995.

Vol. 1011: T. Furuhashi (Ed.), Advances in Fuzzy Logic, Neural Networks and Genetic Algorithms. Proceedings, 1994. VIII, 223 pages. 1995.

Vol. 1020: I. D. Watson (Ed.), Progress in Case-Based Reasoning. Proceedings, 1995. VIII, 209 pages. 1995.

Vol. 1036: G. Adorni, M. Zock (Eds.), Trends in Natural Language Generation. Proceedings, 1993. IX, 382 pages. 1996.

Vol. 1037: M. Wooldridge, J.P. Müller, M. Tambe (Eds.), Intelligent Agents II. Proceedings, 1995. XVI, 437 pages, 1996.

Vol. 1038: W. Van de Velde, J.W. Perram (Eds.), Agents Breaking Away. Proceedings, 1996. XIV, 232 pages, 1996.

Vol. 1040: S. Wermter, E. Riloff, G. Scheler (Eds.), Connectionist, Statistical, and Symbolic Approaches to Learning for Natural Language Processing. IX, 468 pages. 1996.

Vol. 1042: G. Weiß, S. Sen (Eds.), Adaption and Learning in Multi-Agent Systems. Proceedings, 1995. X, 238 pages. 1996.

Vol. 1047: E. Hajnicz, Time Structures. IX, 244 pages. 1996.

Vol. 1050: R. Dyckhoff, H. Herre, P. Schroeder-Heister (Eds.), Extensions of Logic Programming. Proceedings, 1996. VIII, 318 pages. 1996.

Vol. 1053: P. Graf, Term Indexing. XVI, 284 pages. 1996.

Vol. 1056: A. Haddadi, Communication and Cooperation in Agent Systems. XIII, 148 pages. 1996.

Vol. 1069: J.W. Perram, J.-P. Müller (Eds.), Distributed Software Agents and Applications. Proceedings, 1994. VIII, 219 pages. 1996.

Vol. 1071: P. Miglioli, U. Moscato, D. Mundici, M. Ornaghi (Eds.), Theorem Proving with Analytic Tableaux and Related Methods. Proceedings, 1996. X, 330 pages. 1996.

Vol. 1076: K. O'Hara, G. Schreiber, N. Shadbolt (Eds.), Advances in Knowledge Acquisition. Proceedings, 1996. XII, 371 pages. 1996.

Lecture Notes in Computer Science